Praise for
IN THE RED ZONE

"Whether you're Tim Tebow, Colt McCoy, or someone who wants
to tell a friend about Jesus, being purposeful gets results. When it
comes to sharing your faith, Kent Tucker makes it so natural that
you'll know exactly what to say to someone who's in the Red Zone.
Be purposeful and read this book."

—Mike Yorkey
Author of *Playing with Purpose: Tim Tebow*
Coauthor of *Growing Up Colt: A Father, a Son, and a Life in Football*

"Many people in today's world, especially young adults, want the
truth about God. What they've been taught does not meet their
needs or give their lives value and meaning. Kent Tucker offers a
game plan for guiding them into an eternal relationship with the
One who will."

—Josh McDowell
Coauthor of *The Unshakable Truth* and *Broken Yet Accepted*

"*In the Red Zone* uses personal stories and practical suggestions to show believers how to help seekers who are close to the goal. This game plan honors those who don't know Jesus. Instead of putting them on the defense, it shows readers how to help seekers keep moving down the spiritual field toward Christ. I highly recommend this book. It will inspire believers and equip them to share their faith."

—Bill Butterworth
Motivational speaker, author of *The Short List*
and *The Promise of the Second Wind*

"Kent Tucker's *In the Red Zone* is a 'must' for those serious about sharing their faith in Jesus Christ. Using football analogies, Tucker lays out a strategy designed to move 'seekers' forward in establishing a personal relationship with the Lord. Many great illustrations help the reader recognize opportunities, respond to difficult questions and present the truth *in a winsome way*. No 'hard sell' here. Tucker presents more than a formula or system designed to get the desired response. Rather, he illustrates authentic care and logic that opens eyes to the truth and prepares the 'soil' for the work of the Spirit of God."

—Bob Vernon
Assistant Chief of Police (ret.) LAPD
Founder, Pointman Leadership Institute

"God is reaching out to every unbeliever to nudge them toward Christ. Some of them are in the Red Zone of their spiritual journey. *In the Red Zone* provides practical suggestions for identifying those who are open to Christ and then step-by-step suggestions for leading them across the line of faith and helping them to begin following Christ. Kent's approach is winsome, friendly and easy to follow. His personal stories make this process attractive and simple to emulate. I highly recommend it."

—Dr. Charles Arn
President Church Growth, Inc., CA

"*In the Red Zone* is an invaluable training resource designed to equip every Christian to articulate the life-changing message of the Gospel in a clear and compelling way. Kent Tucker's winsome style is easy to understand and emulate. Through step-by-step instruction and real-life examples, believers will learn everything they need to know to help others not only become Christians, but also grow in their newfound faith. Kent has served the Church well by providing this outstanding guide to compassionately walk those in the Red Zone across the line of faith."

—Garry Poole
Strategic planning consultant
Author of numerous resources including *Seeker Small Groups*

"It is often a long journey for someone to come to faith in Christ. But once a seeker has entered the Red Zone of his spiritual journey and is open to God, someone needs to show him how to cross the line of faith. Kent has done a great job of showing us how to do that in a very personal, friendly, and unthreatening way. His practical suggestions and personal stories make this process simple, clear, and easy to learn for the typical group member. This book is a fabulous tool for all small groups."

—Steve Gladen
Author of *Leading Small Groups with Purpose*
Pastor of the Small Group Community, Saddleback Church

"This is one practical 'play-book!' It's user-friendly, a powerful tool that equips believers to understand how their participation can make a difference in the eternal destiny of their friends. Christians need help to learn how to identify seekers in the 'red-zone.' Thank you for your practical approach, gifted insights, and the general encouragement that all of us have a vital piece-of-the-action to see our friends accept Christ and go on to fruitfulness themselves in God's purposes. Thank you, thank you, thank you!"

—Sam Hershey
U.S. International Coordinator, Church Discipleship Ministry,
The Navigators

"With warmth and humor Kent shows Christians how they can share their faith with confidence and conviction. His coaching on how to share your faith is the finest around. I am praying that God will use it to start fires in our churches that will never go out."

—Ray Johnston
Senior Pastor, Bayside Church, CA

"Kent Tucker has an incredible passion and gifting to share the good news of Jesus Christ. And, he has a special ability to encourage and equip others to do the same. This book will help you become more eager and prepared to share God's love in deed and word."

—Paul Cedar
Chairman, Mission America Coalition

"Many books written on evangelism focus on the 'why' of evangelism, but few talk about the 'who' and 'how.' *In the Red Zone* provides all three! In it, Kent explains the motivation behind outreach and offers practical suggestions for identifying those who want help to find God. Plus Kent's step-by-step process equips believers to clearly communicate the Gospel. As the Pastor of Small Groups in a mega church, I especially appreciate the discussion questions provided for each chapter."

—Linda Jones
Pastoral Lead of Community Life,
Water of Life Community Church, CA

Praise for *In the Red Zone*

"It wasn't until someone sat down with me and clearly shared *how* I could begin a relationship with Jesus Christ through the use of a similar bridge illustration that I was able to 'cross the goal-line' so-to-speak and experience new birth in Christ. Kent's book is the best 'game plan' I've ever seen to help Christians share their faith with genuine 'red-zone-seekers.' We are using it in our church and hear nothing but raves about how helpful, practical and powerful this approach is in the power of the Holy Spirit!"

—Roger Bosch
Associate Pastor of Evangelism and Missions,
Lake Avenue Church, Pasadena, CA

"I love to hear our people share stories about leading their friends to Christ because it fulfills the mandate that every believer has from God—duplicating ourselves by making disciples of others. Kent's game plan for identifying seekers open to God and providing an easy way to lead them to Christ has been transformational for our church. The discussion questions for small groups at the end of each chapter have deepened our hearts for the lost and grown our confidence about how to help them. Every believer needs the practical principles that come from this book!"

—Bishop Craig W. Johnson, Th. D.
Senior Pastor, Cathedral of Praise International Ministries,
Rialto, CA

"Kent Tucker is the best at training others to share Jesus. *In the Red Zone* is biblical, relevant, clear, practical and winsome. I especially like his section on questions that propel a conversation in a spiritual direction."

—Michael Risley
Executive Pastor, Voyagers Bible Church, CA

IN THE
RED
ZONE

A GAME PLAN
FOR HOW TO
SHARE YOUR FAITH

DR. KENT TUCKER
WITH **PATTI TOWNLEY-COVERT**

This book is dedicated to my wife, Betsy,
for the countless ways you live out God's love for people.
I am blessed and deeply grateful to have you at my side
and to be able to travel this journey together.

Table of Contents

List of Figures

Foreword

Many have called it the greatest upset in Rose Bowl history. It was not only UCLA's first victory in "The Granddaddy of Them All," the oldest and most prestigious bowl (the 52nd Rose Bowl and UCLA's sixth attempt at a victory), but "The Gutty Little Bruins" turned back the tide on an undefeated Michigan State University, the number #1 team in the nation during that 1965 season. Final score: UCLA 14, MSU 12!

The January 1, 1966 Rose Bowl was won and lost in the "Red Zone," the final twenty yards before the goal line. I know. I was there. Elected by my teammates, I served as the offensive captain during a season in which UCLA was supposed to come in last.

But on that day, UCLA won the game in the Red Zone. From the one yard line, we broke into the end zone and scored two touchdowns.

MSU lost the game in the Red Zone. Their team missed the extra point and their final gasping attempt at a tie fell short of the goal line by two feet.

Dr. Kent Tucker has taken football's "Red Zone" strategy and creatively applied it to personal evangelism: "Red Zone Evangelism." I do not know of any other approach to personal evangelism that comes close to this biblical and practical strategy for sharing our faith with friends, acquaintances, and family members.

I have known Kent for over fifty years and count him as one of my best friends and a fellow-worker in the Gospel. What Kent has written in *In the Red Zone: A Game Plan for How To Share Your Faith*, he has been living himself and using to train others for many years.

As a young Jewish man, I spent eight years bitterly arguing against the good news of the Gospel (outside the Red Zone). Then God placed Kent into my spiritual huddle (inside the Red Zone). Kent knew God had moved me into the Red Zone, when, by the grace of God, my heart began turning toward God. In a matter of weeks, with Kent's assistance and the prayers of many spiritual teammates, I trusted in Jesus Christ as my personal Messiah, Lord, and Savior. To this day, I rejoice in my personal relationship with Jesus. Rose Bowl glory lasted but a few short months. God's forever family lasts forever!

Of all the areas of our Christian lives, sharing our faith with others is probably one of the most fearful. At a time when personal evangelism is most needed, God has raised up Dr. Kent Tucker to help us boldly, lovingly, and accurately share our faith with others, especially when God has moved them into the Red Zone.

Thanks be to God that He has now given us an effective apostolic strategy.

—Dr. Barry R. Leventhal
Former Provost and Academic Dean,
and currently Distinguished Professor
at Southern Evangelical Seminary
Matthews, NC
SES.edu

A Note to Pastors

I wonder if you face the same obstacles I encounter as a pastor. Though you want to equip your church for outreach, finding the right training materials seems almost impossible. Evangelism has become especially tough in a world where many believers shy away from even speaking the name of Jesus.

Well, if you want to train your church to reach out and touch others with the love of Christ, there's great news. Dr. Kent Tucker has not only made equipping for evangelism accessible, he's also made the learning process fun!

Kent has taught his "How To Share Your Faith" game plan to over 500 of our school of ministry students, and it has literally transformed the way they view leading others to Jesus. When I walk across our campus, I frequently encounter individuals who have been led to the Lord or who have led someone else to Christ while using Kent's material. Our secretarial staff has even used Kent's Bridge diagram to lead people in the waiting room to Jesus!

The best way to equip your congregation to share their faith is to encourage them to read *In the Red Zone: A Game Plan for How To Share Your Faith*. It will convince those Christians, who might never otherwise consider evangelism, that they can help their friends, family, coworkers, neighbors, and even strangers cross the line of faith into a personal relationship with Christ.

—Dan Carroll
Senior Pastor
Water of Life Community Church
Fontana, CA

Acknowledgments

With deep gratitude I want to express my thanks to:

- Ben Rodriguez and Brett Hutchinson for casting the vision for a book that tells the story and describes the strategy of Red Zone Evangelism (RZE).

- Doug and Mary Hanks for your encouragement and the time you spent editing my words.

- Barry Leventhal and Steve Zelt for your support, excellent peer review, and guidance.

- Patti Townley-Covert, my coauthor, for your belief in me and the vision and approach of RZE. Thank you for your tireless effort and unfailing devotion toward shaping, editing, and communicating my heart and ministry.

- Sandra Dimas for her superb copy-editing skills.

- Ron Widman for helping create and visually display all the diagrams that explain RZE.

- Jon Price for your outstanding book cover and design.

- Garry Poole for believing so deeply in the Red Zone game plan and your significant contributions, especially the thought-provoking discussion questions.

- the team of pastors, Christian leaders, and people I've been connected with in various groups through the years. Your affirmation, feedback, and encouragement have helped me stay the course, trust God with all my heart, and be a positive influence on others for Christ—then to extend that influence as far as I can.

- all the individuals, whose stories are interwoven with mine in these pages. By sharing your journey, many others will also find their way home to the Savior.

- all the people who have been through the training course at Hillside Community Church and Water of Life Community Church. You've inspired and encouraged me as you've shared your experiences.

- the *How To Share Your Faith* board and friends for your support, wise counsel, personal encouragement, and investment into my life and ministry.

Introduction

The Kick Off

When the Florida Gators ran onto the field, no one could mistake Tim Tebow for somebody else. The eye black etched with John 3:16 differentiated him from the rest of the college players. Tebow showed no fear when it came to sharing his Christian faith.

In his book, *Through My Eyes*, Tebow said:

> I have learned that, though God is in control of the big picture, I am responsible for how I use my platform, whatever its size— at this moment in time—to influence others. Or whatever my age. Or wherever I am, or no matter what is going on in my life at any time. I have a platform that He can use for His good purposes and perhaps even the good of others—today. (p. x)

Though every Christian has a platform, few have one the size of Tim Tebow's. Yet, regardless of the size of our platform, the thought of sharing our faith often produces anxiety in many of us. The question is why? Why does the thought of sharing our faith produce so much anxiety in so many believers?

The Bible commands us to "go into all the world and preach the good news to all creation" (Mark 16:15), yet the very thought of the "E" word raises so many issues that most of us dismiss it. Some Christians (and many nonbelievers) even consider evangelism a dirty word.

There may be good reason. Have you ever watched a football game where your favorite team can't complete a pass or gets blocked at every turn? You may have even shouted at the television—"What's the matter with you!" The problems may involve poor coaching, poor skills, or not enough practice. Or, perhaps the team is completely outmatched.

Similar issues have taken their toll on many Christians. Have you ever tried to share your faith and gotten so bruised and battered in the process that you stopped making the effort? Or maybe you don't even try because you don't know what to say, how to say it, or when.

Red Zone Evangelism

That was my problem when I first joined UCLA's football team; I simply didn't know what to say. At least not until I developed a game plan to share my faith—one that's as dynamic as any football game (see chapter 1).

Perhaps that's because football fueled the ideas behind Red Zone Evangelism (RZE). To equip a team to win, coaches diagram specific plays giving them memorable names. Then the team practices various options until they build confidence about what to do, how to do it, and when. In real-time, after the quarterback calls that play, it becomes unique and adaptable depending on each individual's circumstances. But the basics remain the same. And, it doesn't matter who is in what position, the goal never changes—to score a touchdown.

The best place to do that is in the "Red Zone." That's the last twenty yards before a player scores. Once a ball carrier or receiver reaches that place, he's ready to go all the way.

"Red Zone" can apply to any situation where someone is close to his goal. In football, that's a touchdown. A major department store holds Red Zone sales to signify that a shopper will find the bargain she's looking for. In evangelism, being in the Red Zone means that someone's heart is turning toward God. The Lord has drawn that person down life's playing field until he is close to entering into a personal relationship with Jesus Christ. Yet, the seeker usually needs someone (or perhaps a team of people) to assist in that drive across the goal line.

Over the years, I've been fascinated with how people come to Christ. My interest began at UCLA and continued to grow while I attended Dallas Theological Seminary. At Fuller Theological Seminary, I pursued my doctorate in Evangelism and Church Growth.

Afterwards, I became a pastor and trained believers to share their faith for more than 40 years. Then, when a large church in Southern California asked me to focus on Evangelism Training, that effort took on added dimensions. My responsibilities became a stepping-stone to "How To Share Your Faith" (HTSYF) seminars. Conducting those training camps became my full-time occupation in 2010.

Within that context, the imagery of RZE has become a useful frame of reference or metaphor for learning to recognize someone ready to hear the good news (chapter 2). Once those seekers have been identified, the Bridge diagram provides the means to present a clear and compelling explanation of the Gospel. Chapters 3–6 describe how to use the diagram and offer memorable key words to remind believers of what to say when.

Biblical coaching sessions throughout the book show how Jesus and His followers interacted with people in the Red Zone of their spiritual journey. Insights from their encounters keep believers off a defensive position and place them on the offense—helping their unsaved friends gain valuable spiritual ground.

The Thrill of Victory

Perhaps you know someone whose mother is dying of cancer. Or maybe your friend feels empty as though life has no purpose. Or your coworker may be getting a divorce and is desperate for advice. You'll find stories of people like these woven throughout this book. Each was in the "Red Zone," ready to score an eternal home.

Though each story illuminates at least one specific point, they are told in their entirety because real people need real help. Intriguing insights gleaned from these true stories will equip you with the responses you've longed for. Chapters 7–10 develop extra training tips designed to show you how to become even more effective as your own stories unfold.

HTSYF training camps have used RZE in 49 states and 15 foreign countries to build the confidence and equip thousands of believers to share the good news with those they care about. Many of the stories included in this book come from those seminars. The names of people and a few insignificant details have been changed to guard the privacy of those involved. But, in essence, each story actually happened as described.

RZE offers Christians insights on how to share their faith in a way that makes a difference. No matter your age, ethnicity, or profession, this game plan for seekers close to the goal will help you make the most of your platform.

Discussion Questions

1. What's motivating you to read and study *In the Red Zone*?
   What insights do you hope to gain from this book about
   sharing your faith?

2. How might discussing the principles conveyed in this book inspire
   you to apply them in your life on an ongoing basis? What are the
   advantages of discussing this content with others in a group setting
   versus thinking about them on your own?

3. Why do you think the idea of sharing the Gospel with nonbelievers
   produces so much anxiety in so many believers?

4. What fears do you have when it comes to sharing your faith
   with others?

5. On a scale from 1–10, regarding sharing your faith, how well do
   you know what to say, how to say it, and when?

6. How important is it to be able to recognize when someone is ready
   to hear the Gospel? Brainstorm what specific signs or indicators
   convey when a person is in the Red Zone.

1

Getting into the Evangelistic Game

A s a sixth grader, I could frequently be found on the football field practicing the rudiments of the game. Sweat made me smelly. Grime caked my face and my socks, and grass stains smeared my pants. My friends and I talked tough about rival teams and our coach focused on strategies for how to beat them in afterschool games. I loved it.

When Steven was eleven-years-old, he may have wished he'd been playing in my cleats. Instead he fought a much tougher battle—cancer. Antiseptic smells permeated his playing field. He wore the uniform of the sick, a thin hospital gown tied at the neck. Rather than growing strong and building muscles, he lay weak and fragile in a hospital bed.

A brain tumor was killing Steven. And, when I met him, he was about to die.

Friends of mine had asked me to go with them to comfort Steven's family as their beloved son and brother lay in a coma. But when we arrived at the hospital, Steven was awake—alert, talking and responding to his parents.

Sometimes just before death, the body rallies with a burst of energy. Sensing that's what was happening, I wondered if Steven knew the Lord and asked his parents if he'd ever prayed to receive Christ as his Savior. They weren't sure. With their encouragement, I sat close by Steven's bed and leaned in so he could hear me.

Quickly, I began sketching a simple diagram (see chapter 3) on the back of a letter-sized envelope I'd found in the bedside drawer. That image showed Steven how to have a personal relationship with Jesus, so he'd know for certain he'd be going to heaven. When I finished the explanation, Steven's dad asked his son if he wanted me to lead him in a prayer to receive Christ. Steven said "yes."

After we prayed, I used simple terms to review God's promises, and it was clear this young boy understood he'd been forgiven. He had absolute assurance that when he closed his eyes for the last time on Earth, he'd open them again in the presence of Jesus.

Within the next few days, Steven slid back into his coma and never regained consciousness. How could it be that Steven had regained consciousness just in time to accept Christ and guarantee he'd be going home to heaven? Why did I "just happen" to be in the right place at the right time?

Jesus cared about the eternal destiny of an eleven-year-old boy. And because I'd learned how easy it can be to share my faith, I knew exactly how to help him step across the goal line into a personal relationship with his Savior. But that wasn't always the case.

Moving Off the Bench

During my first year at UCLA, despite being red-shirted, football was what I cared about most. Until the weekend my fraternity brother, Carl, went home and never came back. He'd been killed in a tragic car crash. And, I felt guilty because I never mentioned the importance of a personal relationship with Jesus.

Like many Christians I simply didn't know what to say, when, or how to say it.

Why do believers, who genuinely love Jesus Christ, have such a hard time sharing their faith?

Bestselling author and world-class evangelist Rebecca Manley Pippert offered these insights in her endorsement for *The Sacrament of Evangelism* by Jerry Root and Stan Guthrie:

> Having taught evangelism around the world I have discovered that the fears are remarkably the same: *What if I offend? What if I'm rejected? What if they ask me a question I can't answer?* However, over time I realized that the deeper, unspoken fear was the assumption that evangelism is ultimately all about us and our skills.

At the time of Carl's death, I didn't fully understand the reasons why I didn't share my faith. All I knew was that it was too late.

If Carl didn't know Jesus, my friend is spending eternity in hell. Carl's destiny is permanent, irreversible, and very bad (2 Thessalonians 1:8–9; Revelation 20:15). If I were somehow transported to hell to visit him, what could I possibly say if he asked, "Why didn't you tell me?" What possible response would satisfy him?

- "I didn't want to offend you."

- "I was afraid of what you'd think of me."

- "I didn't want to lose your friendship."

- "I felt like a hypocrite because you know all the stuff I've done."

- "I've never learned how to explain what I believe."

- "Evangelism isn't my gift."

With such inadequate excuses I could envision Carl in his torment asking, "Why didn't you take a 2' x 4' and hit me over the head with it?" The problem is that wouldn't have worked.

Those thoughts revealed disturbing things about me. I hadn't really cared what was best for my friend. If I had, I'd have been more concerned about the long-term benefits of eternal life. There's no way I'd have permitted my own insecurities to keep me from sharing my faith. But that didn't eliminate my fears or equip me with what to say.

Carl's death instigated a personal challenge to find solutions to these problems. The need to tell people about Jesus became more:

- *urgent* as I realized that anyone can die at any time.

- *intense* as I came to understand that Satan does not want people to know Christ. And,

- *serious.* The results of sharing my faith (or not) have eternal significance.

So I began a quest to figure out how any Christian, regardless of giftedness, could share his faith in an easy, natural, and effective way.

That's what Jesus asked His followers to do. All four Gospels end with a clear, passionate command for believers to "Go" share the gospel (Matthew 28:19–20; Mark 16:15; Luke 24:46–49; John 20:21). Jesus didn't exclude anyone from that directive. The question was how? How can anyone share their faith in a way that builds relationships up instead of tearing them down?

Discussion Questions

1. To what extent does God care about the eternal destiny of every person? Give reasons for your response.

2. What impact would it make on your life if you could say with confidence you know how to help others come to Christ?

3. To what extent can you relate to common fears about sharing your faith such as: What if I offend? What if I'm rejected? What if they ask me a question I can't answer? What insecurities prevent you from sharing your faith?

4. To what extent can you relate to Kent's story about how he didn't share his faith with his friend Carl, who died? What does it convey about the urgency of the Gospel? How does this reality motivate or discourage you?

5. To what extent do you think Christians are responsible for sharing the Gospel? How might we strike a balance between living with the urgency of sharing our faith, yet not assuming full responsibility for the eternal destiny of others?

6. Kent confessed that he hadn't really cared what was best for his friend. What are some things we can do to raise our level of concern for people who don't know Christ?

7. Why is it important to share your faith in a way that builds relationships up instead of tearing them down? What ideas do you have for how to make that happen?

2

Finding the
Right Receiver

Years of football experience have convinced me that the best way to score is to get the ball into the hands of an open receiver. It's that simple. The quarterback needs to look for someone who's open and aim for him. There's not much point in going to those who aren't.

Long runs and completed passes make for thrilling plays and sometimes lead to a touchdown. But far more often simply moving the football down the field, one play at a time, leads to a score. Especially when a team enters the "Red Zone."

Once they get inside that twenty-yard line, the game intensifies. Strategic plays are called and executed. All eyes are on one thing—the goal line.

In a similar way, seekers often face a long drive to come to Christ. During that process, they might encounter huge obstacles. But when God has been working in someone's life and he reaches the special place where he's spiritually open, senses something is missing in his life, and wonders if Christ can help; he is in the Red Zone of his spiritual journey (see figure 2.1).

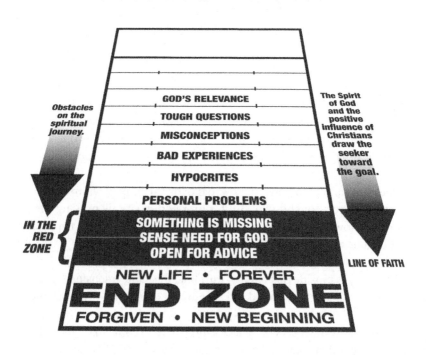

Figure 2.1. The Red Zone Evangelism Diagram. RZE identifies individuals close to the goal, who need help to cross the line of faith into a personal relationship with Jesus Christ.

Being in the Red Zone made all the difference for my friend Barry Leventhal. Though God had been pursuing him for years, he had no interest because he was not yet in the Red Zone. He was focused on football and didn't think about much else. Determined to achieve five career goals, my friend intended to:

1) play football for UCLA in, what was then, the Pac-8 Conference,
2. be captain of UCLA's offense in his senior year,
3. win the Pac-8 Conference,
4. play in the Rose Bowl, and
5. win the Rose Bowl game.

Barry accomplished all five of these objectives during his senior year. The Rose Bowl game capped off a thrilling season. On the final play of the game, UCLA scored, beating the undefeated number one team in the nation, Michigan State. The final score was UCLA 14, MSU 12. Yet, in spite of this great accomplishment, within a couple months he was dejected. Achieving his goals had not given him the sense of fulfillment he wanted. Something was still missing.

Barry had entered the Red Zone. For the first time, he became open to talking about Jesus.

Another friend and I started talking with Barry about the difference Jesus could make, and it didn't take long before he received Christ. After that his life took on new spiritual significance—one that led to full-time pastoral ministry. Eventually he served as provost, academic dean, and currently as "distinguished professor" of the Southern Evangelical Seminary in Matthews, North Carolina.

The idea of trying to find out where people are on their spiritual journey has been around for hundreds of years. Perhaps the reason many Christians have recognized the importance of determining a person's readiness before trying to help someone across the goal line of faith is because that's the approach Jesus and the apostles used.

Biblical Coaching Sessions

There's no doubt Christ offers forgiveness and eternal life to every individual. John 3:16 clearly states "God so loved the world that He gave His one and only Son, that whoever believes in Him shall not perish but have eternal life." However, Jesus and His disciples didn't focus on everyone. They didn't lavish time on the rich. Or on political figures or religious leaders. Rather Jesus spent time talking with those individuals who were open.

Christ

Jesus focused on those who recognized their need for God and His forgiveness. He paid special attention to the Roman centurion (Matthew 8:5–13), a wealthy man named Zacchaeus (Luke 19:1–9), and the Samaritan woman (John 4:1–42), among many others. Each of these people willingly acknowledged their need for forgiveness and desire for a better life.

Despite being criticized for His association with such unseemly characters, Jesus took time for them because of their responsiveness to Him. He explained this strategy in Luke 5:31. "It is not the healthy who need a doctor, but the sick. I have not come to call the righteous but sinners to repentance."

Paul

These were also the types of people the Apostle Paul set out to meet. When he traveled to other countries, he sought out individuals whose minds, circumstances, and relationships were drawing them closer to Christ.

Most people responsive to God hung out in the synagogues and participated in spiritual discussions. So Paul's game plan involved going there to talk about Jesus and explain that His resurrection from the dead proved He was who He claimed to be—the Son of God, the Savior of the world (see Acts 13, 14, 17, 18, and 19). Those truly seeking God came to believe in Christ and began meeting with Paul to learn more. Sometimes the unbelieving Jews hardened their resistance, forcing Paul out of the synagogue. But that didn't stop him. Instead, he went to find those who were spiritually responsive and helped them start new churches.

In Philippi, a city without a synagogue, Paul looked for the place where those seeking God might meet. "On the Sabbath," he said they "went outside the city gate to the river, where we expected to find a place of prayer" (Acts 16:13a). Some women were gathered there, so Paul shared the good news. The Lord opened Lydia's heart and she responded to Paul's message (Acts 16:14). Lydia was in the Red Zone and crossed the line of faith.

Assessing Spiritual Receptivity

Jesus always knows the condition of individual human hearts, but for His followers trying to figure that out can prove more challenging. William Wilberforce (1759–1833) approached this issue with great deliberation:

> Everywhere he went, and with everyone he met, he tried, as best he could, to bring the conversation around to the question of eternity. Wilberforce prepared lists of his friends and next to their names he made notes on how he might best encourage them in their faith, if they were believers, and to know Christ if they were not. He listed subjects to bring up with each individual that might launch a conversation about spiritual issues. He described these subjects and questions as 'launchers' and was always looking for opportunities to introduce them. (*Amazing Grace: William Wilberforce and the Heroic Campaign to End Slavery in the British Empire* by Eric Metaxas, p. 167)

Though spiritual discussions can be far more spontaneous, the best way to discover a person's beliefs is simply to take an interest in them. Strategic questions about their lives can easily reveal what a Christian needs to know.

Launchers

Over the years, I've learned to ask questions that propel a conversation in a spiritual direction. These questions usually help me find out if a person is in the Red Zone.

- *"When I think of you, how can I pray for you?"* This question lets someone know I'm thinking of him even when we're not together. It makes him feel cared about, and I genuinely do care.

  If the response is "pray any way you want," then that person is probably not very receptive. But if he begins to talk about the real concerns in his life, then there's an open door to learn more about his spiritual journey. When an individual shares about his personal needs or struggles, it connects us in a way that generally leads to deeper discussions the next time we meet.

- *"What is your church background?"* Asking about church background is less threatening than asking, "Are you a Christian? Do you go to church?" Or, "What church do you attend?" When I ask about a person's church background, I'm asking about her history, her background, her parents' religious influence, her upbringing and so forth.

  This question accomplishes the same purpose with people from diverse spiritual backgrounds, as the word "church" supplies a Christian context and avoids complicating matters with other religious beliefs.

As an individual shares about his experiences, I follow up with questions about what has happened on his journey since then and where he is today.

(a) "Are you at a place in your spiritual life where you can say for certain that if you die tonight you'll go to heaven?" Everyone has a spiritual life, so it's natural to ask such a question. Some people admit they're not certain. However, most people believe they are going to heaven. They may not be absolutely sure, but feel good about the probability.

Regardless of how someone answers this question, it moves the conversation toward the subject of heaven. That sets up question "b."

(b) "If you die tonight and God asks, 'Why should I let you into My heaven?'—what will you say?" That's a key question. The answer reveals what an individual is trusting to get him into heaven. If he responds that he has received Christ, I rejoice with him. But if he says he's been a good person or talks about his good works, I respond by saying, "That's a good answer, but there's a better one. May I show it to you?"

A spiritually responsive person is usually open to talking about these things. If he shuts down the conversation or changes the subject, it may be an indicator that he is not in the Red Zone.

It's important to respect where a person is on his spiritual journey and avoid being pushy. That turns people off and ends the discussion.

- **"What is the high point and low point of your week?"** This is a stimulating "get-acquainted" or "catch-up" question. People can answer at any level they feel comfortable with, but they often go below the surface, especially if they sense you have a genuine interest. It is often best for you to answer the question first and be vulnerable. That will set a tone that helps them feel more comfortable confiding in you.

- **"If you could ask God one question you knew he would answer right away, what would it be?"** I often use this question from Garry Poole's book *The Complete Book of Questions, #1001* with seekers and new believers because it reveals significant issues, hurts, or struggles that result in distrust toward God. Then I can address those questions in a way that will help them draw closer to God.

Ready Receivers

The answers to these questions usually take ordinary conversations in a spiritually significant direction. A visit to the dry cleaners, a social event, and a dental appointment show how they can identify people in the Red Zone.

A Visit to the Dry Cleaners. One day, while running errands, I took some dry cleaning in and dropped it off at the front counter. While there I started talking with the owner's wife. On the spur of the moment, I asked Fatima, "When I think of you, how do you want me to pray for you?" She immediately said, "Pray for our business and my health."

So I asked about her health, and she said, "There is a history of heart problems in my family. Mine was beating fast, and it wouldn't stop. The ER doctor did some tests and said it was stress. I'm very stressed about our business."

When I asked if she prayed, she responded softly, "Yes."

"Do you read the Bible," I asked.

Again she said "Yes," but explained that her niece gave her a Jehovah's Witnesses booklet about the Bible, and she was actually reading that.

The next time I saw Fatima, I gave her a Bible and suggested she begin reading the Gospel of John. I also handed her a little gospel tract on how to know God personally. A few days later, when I went to pick up my cleaning, Fatima said she'd already finished the Gospel of John and was halfway through the Gospel of Matthew. She had also read the gospel tract and asked Christ into her heart.

Her answers to a few more questions demonstrated that she had a solid understanding of the Gospel. Now, I see her often, and she continues to grow spiritually, finding God's help and peace about her business. She has become a real blessing to me, and it all started with the question, "When I think of you, how do you want me to pray?"

A variation of that question—"Do you pray and ask God to help you?"— is a good one to ask when someone mentions going through difficult times. Often that will lead to the question about their church background. One question leading to another begins moving the proverbial ball down the field and often identifies someone who is in the Red Zone.

A Social Event. Some time ago, I met a young man named Robert and his fiancée at a charity event. Robert was bald from chemotherapy. So was my wife. With that common ground we started chatting about cancer. Despite having twenty-six tumors in his own body, Robert was attending the cancer event to support a friend.

During our conversation, I asked Robert about his church background. He said he didn't really have one, so I asked, "Are you in the place in your spiritual life where, you know for certain if you die, you'll go to heaven?"

He shook his head, and immediately tears ran down his cheeks. His fiancée also started to cry.

So I asked, "If you die tonight and God asks you, 'Why should I let you into My heaven,' what will you say?" He just shook his head again and more tears fell.

Recognizing a divine appointment I assured Robert, "I can help you with that." We found a table, sat down, and I drew out a simple diagram. Then, I led both Robert and his fiancée in a prayer to receive Jesus.

They were in the Red Zone. A simple question—"What is your church background?"—enabled me to learn about their spiritual journey and where they were in a relationship with God.

As Robert described his spiritual history, I followed-up with questions about what had happened on his journey since then and where he is today. Being spiritually responsive made him open to talk about such things. But if he had evaded the question or changed the subject, I likely would have decided he was not in the Red Zone, and it was time to back off.

A Dental Appointment. "What is the high point and low point of your week?" I asked the dental hygienist. Her eyes filled with tears as she said that her 1-1/2 year-old daughter was going to have surgery on her bladder. I found out that the frightened mom was already a Christian, so I prayed for her right then, asking for God's mercy and healing for her daughter.

My next appointment was with the dental assistant. On that occasion, we both shared our answers to that same question. She, too, was a Christian. Dealing with her ex-husband and the wound their divorce left on her and her son was her low point. She was vulnerable about her struggle and grateful when I suggested we pray together.

An Individualized Game Plan

Asking questions to identify where a person is on their spiritual journey can provide insights into how God may already be working in that person's life. Rebecca Pippert wrote that when it comes to evangelism,

> we suck up our courage and just hope that God will back us up! But we've got it backwards. God always goes before us because He is already there. We follow Him into the world, He doesn't follow us. Evangelism is cooperating with what God is already doing! (Endorsement for *The Sacrament of Evangelism* by Jerry Root and Stan Guthrie.)

In his book, *The Unexpected Adventure*, Lee Strobel concurred. He said:

> Evangelism is never a solo activity. God is always working behind the scenes to draw people to himself. And one of the greatest thrills in sharing our faith is to catch occasional glimpses of his covert activity. It's almost as if he's winking at us and saying, "You ain't seen nothin' yet. Stick with me and I'll show you some 'divine coincidences' that will rock your world and exponentially expand your faith." (p. 248)

In the normal course of a day, Christians encounter people with a wide variety of responses toward spiritual issues. Some have been quietly turning toward God in their hearts. They have been coming closer and closer to God. Those around them may not even be aware of that, but God is. He knows who they are and where they are. God knows what will touch their hearts and who can provide the assistance they need to cross the line of faith. The next chapter shows an effective way to offer that type of help.

Discussion Questions

1. Jesus and His disciples spent the most time talking to those who were spiritually open. How might His example apply (or not) to your evangelistic efforts.

2. Kent frequently says that once a seeker "reaches the special place where he's spiritually open, senses something is missing in his life, and wonders if Christ can help; he's in the Red Zone of his spiritual journey." What are some other traits or characteristics that reveal someone who is in the Red Zone?

3. Why is it important to determine a person's readiness before trying to help her across the goal line of faith? What are some things you could do to help increase that individual's readiness to receive Christ?

4. In what way might asking someone how you could pray for him reveal where that individual is spiritually? Is this a nonthreatening question? Why or why not?

5. In Kent's story about a visit to the dry cleaners, he asked the "launcher" question: "When I think of you, how do you want me to pray for you?" Give an example of ways you might ask someone that question this week?

6. In the Bible, Paul sought out individuals whose minds, circumstances, and relationships were drawing them closer to Christ. Who in your sphere of influence is drawing near to Christ right now? After you share, take a few moments to pray for them. (At the end of each chapter, after considering the discussion questions, take a few minutes to share and pray for the people you know who are in the Red Zone.)

3

Putting the Playbook into Action

In 1983, Joe Gibbs led the Washington Redskins to their first NFL championship in four decades. It was only his second year as the head coach. The Redskins also won Super Bowl XXII in 1988 and Super Bowl XXVI in 1992—three NFL championships in 10 seasons.

Gibbs described the importance of being strategic in his book, *Game Plan for Life*:

> When our players came to Redskins Park on Wednesday, we'd hand each one a two-inch-thick binder that would have everything they'd need to know about the other team and the plays and formations we'd be running. Throughout the rest of the week, we'd start to specify certain plays for certain situations—short yardage, goal line, third down priority plays, and so on.
>
> By the end of the week, we'd have the game plan developed down to the exact plays and formations we'd run in every situation. *Nothing was left to chance.* (p. 6)

That binder included hundreds of plays and dozens of formations so the best one could be used depending on the circumstance. The Redskins playbook even divided the last twenty yards before the goal into five-yard increments. It described specific plays for each segment in the Red Zone.

When it comes to faith-sharing, the stakes are much higher than they are in any football game. A person's salvation, transformation, purpose, influence, marriage, family, and eternal destiny all depend on a personal relationship with Jesus Christ. Because of that—God calls, exhorts, and commands believers to be intentional about being prepared to share their faith with those who are in the Red Zone of their spiritual journey.

A Simple Strategy

How To Share Your Faith's (HTSYF) game plan works. It's proven effective with Christians from grade-school kids to the elderly—from new believers to those who have walked with Jesus for many years. Plus, it equips those who don't have the gift of evangelism with the confidence they need to share their faith.

RZE uses natural conversation starters (see chapter 2) to assess an individual's receptivity. Once a person's open to hearing about Jesus, it's time to present the Gospel in a clear, compelling way. In his book *Just Walk Across the Room*, Bill Hybels claimed that the best approach to communicating this life-altering experience is to use pictures. He said he relies on one illustration in particular—the "Bridge." So does HTSYF.

Alex, a high school girl who attended one of our four-week training camps, discovered for herself how God could use this simple diagram with her friends.

A Spiritual Victory

One day at school Alex, a teacher's aide, decided to go out in the deserted hallway to grade papers. Soon after this petite dark-haired girl sat down on the floor, her new friend Dominic happened to walk by. As they started chatting, he brought up a mutual acquaintance.

"Allena's like super nice to me now," he said. "Why's she so different?"

"Hmmm, I don't know, maybe it's because she became a Christian." Alex teased.

"So, how did you become a Christian?" Dominic asked.

Alex responded with a condensed version of her testimony. Obviously touched, Dominic seemed so receptive that Alex asked if she could show him a diagram she'd learned that shows how someone can become a Christian.

To her surprise, Dominic agreed. So Alex found a scrap of paper and used her grading pen to draw the Bridge diagram shown in figure 3.1.

As she drew, Alex described the relationship God desires to have with people, the way sin separates people from Him, and the good works individuals perform to try and get right with God. She showed Dominic that no matter how hard a person tries, he'll always fall short. Then she described how God gave His only Son to save anyone who receives Him.

After Alex finished, Dominic said he wanted to receive Christ as his Lord and Savior. Sitting there on the tiled floor, leaning against the brick walls, Alex led Dominic through a simple prayer to express his faith in Christ. She experienced the thrill of helping him move from the spiritual Red Zone across the line of faith.

Figure 3.1. The Bridge Diagram. This bridge diagram is easy to draw and an effective way to present the Gospel. ©2013 Share Your Faith Ministries, Inc. All rights reserved.

The reason this diagram worked so well was because God had already been working in Dominic's heart to bring him into a place of readiness. Alex recognized a providential opening and seized the opportunity to assist with Dominic's spiritual conversion.

A Clear and Compelling Presentation

A diagram similar to the one Alex drew has been around for decades. Originally developed by the Navigators, they called their presentation the "Bridge to Life." In their book, *Becoming a Contagious Christian*, Bill Hybels and Mark Mittelberg said the Bridge "is probably the best-known and most frequently used gospel illustration around, and for good reason. It graphically shows people their predicament and God's solution" (p. 156).

I elaborated on the Bridge concept by adding memorable words to my diagram that can easily be adapted to make the explanation more personal. Drawing out this diagram engages people like Dominic every step of the way. It communicates much more personally and powerfully than any other method I've ever seen.

A picture really can be worth a thousand words. And, this one does not require any artistic skills. Even crooked lines sketched on a scrap of note-book paper illustrate the Gospel in a simple, clear, and compelling way.

Drawing the Bridge

The Bridge is nonthreatening and, when drawn step-by-step, explains humanity's situation and what God has done for each individual. Alex learned to present it in three parts and you can too. Think of a sandwich—the opening and concluding questions form the two slices of bread. The meat (or diagram) is in the middle.

Alex started with the meat of the message using key words to help her remember what to say. Figure 3.2 shows the progression. Individual parts of the diagram (in the left column) correspond to key words (in the right column).

Those key words also helped Dominic grasp the concepts (see figure 3.3 for examples).

Each key word association reinforces *how* to communicate the message. For example, when Alex wrote "Us" and "God," the key word "Relationship," triggered the thought of how to use it in a sentence. She could have said, "God wants a relationship with us." Or "God loves us and wants a relationship with us." Or "God created us so He could have a personal relationship with us." Alex put each sentence explaining the diagram in her own words so there was no script to memorize. Using familiar language made the presentation genuine. Being honest and real makes the information trustworthy. The key word was simply a tool to keep her on track.

An Opening Question

A sandwich doesn't exist without the bread. Though RZE depends on the Bridge to show seekers the importance of a personal relationship with Jesus; to be considered, it must be introduced into the conversation. An easy question started Alex's discussion with Dominic.

"Someone showed me a simple diagram that reveals how someone can get closer to God. May I show it to you?"

This concept could be said in many different ways depending on the interest of the seeker. One friend may be concerned about the stress in her life. A family member may fear death. A new acquaintance may be lonely.

"Someone showed me a simple diagram that helped me understand how to have:

- eternal life."
- peace with God."
- a personal relationship with Jesus."

That phrase in the middle can be tailored to each individual situation. But *"Someone showed me a simple diagram... May I show it to you?"* are the key phrases that move the conversation down the field.

If Dominic's response and/or body language had revealed that this question made him uncomfortable, Alex could have whispered a prayer and asked for God's words and wisdom to bring the right words. When someone is not in the Red Zone, being patient, kind, and gentle may pave the way for future discussions.

But, when a person expresses interest like Dominic did—it's time to go for it. Alex sketched the Bridge and explained the Gospel, just the way she'd been taught.

Concluding Questions

After drawing the Bridge, Alex asked three concluding questions to lead Dominic into a response.

1. *"Does this make sense?"* Dominic's affirmative response set up the next question. (Having used the Bridge diagram for several years, I can honestly say I've never had anyone claim it doesn't make sense. So the answer to this question will likely be "yes." If for some reason it's not, the next question would be "What part did not make sense to you?" A little clarification might help.)

BRIDGE DIAGRAM	KEY WORDS
US GOD	**Relationship**
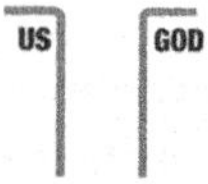 US GOD	**Separation**
 US GOD	**Good Works**
 US GOD	**Fall Short**
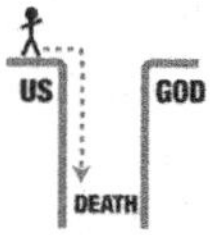 US GOD DEATH	**Death**
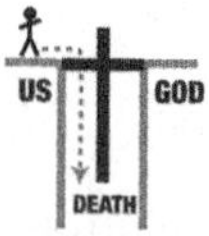 US GOD DEATH	**Bridge**
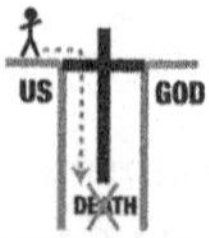 US GOD DEATH	**Paid**
 Receive Christ US GOD DEATH	**Receive**

Figure 3.2. A Step-by-Step Presentation of the Bridge Diagram Using Key Words.
Memorizing key words makes the process of presenting the Good News easy to remember.

BRIDGE DIAGRAM	USE THE KEY WORDS IN A SENTENCE
US GOD	God loves us and wants to have a **relationship** with us.
US GOD	However, we have chosen to go our own independent way and our sins have caused a **separation** between us and God.
US GOD	Most of us are aware of this separation, and we try to do **good works** to get back to God.
US GOD	But no one is perfect. We all sin and **fall short** of God's standard.
US GOD DEATH	The Bible says the penalty for our sins is **death** (spiritual separation from God).
US GOD DEATH	But God did for us what we could not do for ourselves. He provided a **bridge** to help us get back to God.
US GOD DEATH	When Jesus Christ died on the cross, he **paid** the penalty for our sins and rose again to be our Savior.
Receive Christ US GOD DEATH	But it is not enough just to know this. To cross over the bridge, we need to **receive** Christ by asking Him to forgive us and come into our lives.

Figure 3.3. Sentences Using Key Words. Sample sentences give the key words a context. Sentences can be easily personalized.

2. **"Where are you?"** or **Where do you see yourself on this diagram?"** By asking this question, Alex wasn't judging Dominic or telling him his spiritual status. Dominic himself described it. He was on the left side of the Bridge.

So Alex asked:

3. **"Would you like to receive Christ and cross over?"** Because she was talking with someone in the Red Zone, Dominic said yes, he wanted to receive Christ. The three key questions had led him closer and closer to the goal.

The concluding questions are:

1. *Make sense?*
2. *Where are you?*
3. *Cross over?*

The three circles on the diagram in figure 3.4 helped Alex visualize and remember these questions.

Straight Down the Middle

The list in figure 3.5 puts this strategic formation together and a clear and compelling presentation of the Gospel results—one that you can use as easily as Alex did.

Quite often, after seeing the Bridge diagram, the individual comprehends for the first time the enormity of what God has done and the meaning of salvation.

This depiction embodies the essence of John 3:16—the central Bible verse that explains the good news. "For God so loved the world that he gave his one and only Son that whoever believes in him shall not perish but have eternal life." (See figure 3.6.)

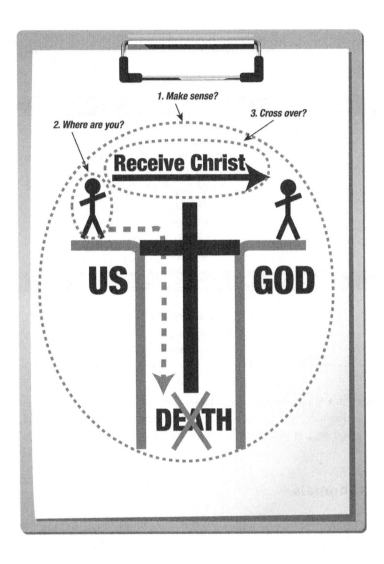

Figure 3.4. The Circle Diagram of the Three Concluding Questions. The largest circle surrounds the entire illustration—because the question is, "Does this whole explanation *make sense*?" The circle of the guy on the left represents the seeker's spiritual status— he's being asked, *"Where are you?"* The arrow and "receive Christ" are circled because the question is: "Would you like to receive Christ and *cross over*?"

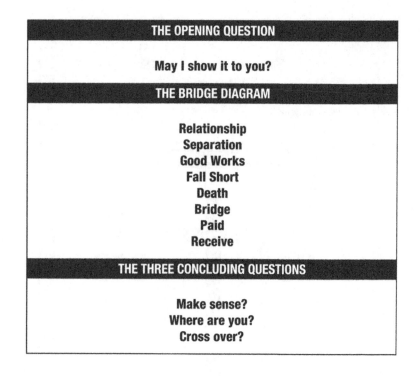

Figure 3.5. A Simple Explanation. These key words along with the Bridge diagram, combined with the opening and concluding questions, lead seekers forward and place them within range of scoring a relationship with Christ.

Testimonials

Football players love to tell football stories. So do those who use RZE. Nothing's more thrilling than seeing someone come to Christ:

Heather: "I practiced drawing out the Bridge with my son. I thought for sure he knew this, but there was a lot he didn't know. For example, he thought he would go back and forth on both sides of the bridge depending on his behavior each day. I explained what Christ had done

Figure 3.6. The Bridge Depicts John 3:16. Sometimes people think Scripture should be added to the diagram, but that's not necessary.

for us and that once we receive Christ, He will never leave us. So last night, I led my son into an everlasting relationship with Christ."

Sean: "I was talking with my coworker about God when she mentioned that she'd always wanted to receive Christ, but didn't know how. So I said, 'I've learned this little diagram, *may I show it to you?*' I explained it to her and asked *'Where do you see yourself on it?'* She said she was over on the left side. I asked if she wanted to *receive Christ right now and cross over.* She did! I led her through the prayer to receive Christ and she became misty-eyed. It was cool!"

Cathy: "I talked to my two sons tonight. I thought they understood because I always talk to them. But drawing out the Bridge diagram made it clear. They got it. I have never led anyone to Christ, and tonight I got to lead my two sons to Him!"

Ben: "My wife and I were lying in bed, and I was telling her how exciting this class was. I am a baby Christian and still learning. She was on the outside looking in. I was going through my study of the *How To Share Your Faith* material and she said 'explain it to me.' So I drew it out and said, 'Do you get it?' She said, 'Yes, I get it.' I told her the benefits of receiving Christ. She cried, and I cried when we prayed together and she received Jesus."

Marilyn: "I didn't think this Bridge diagram would work. It was just too simple. But then I was talking with a lady about scrapbooking supplies, and we started talking about God. She said she had been going to a Bible study but didn't get it. I showed her the Bridge diagram. She wanted to *cross over.* I led her in prayer to receive Christ. It was awesome! Now, I know the Bridge really works. It may be simple, but it is very effective."

Each of these believers talked with people in the Red Zone of their spiritual journey. Those who knew how to share their faith, helped seeking individuals score the ultimate goal: a personal relationship with Jesus Christ. But along the way, those seasoned Christians may have encountered some opposition. Chapter 4 shows how to field questions when you don't know the answers.

Discussion Questions

1. When it comes to evangelism, how important is a strategy? What does it mean to be strategic from an evangelistic perspective?

2. God challenges believers to be prepared to share their faith with those who are in the Red Zone. In what areas do you feel strong and/or inadequate? What are some ways you could become better prepared to share your faith?

3. Share a story of a time you attempted to use an illustration to share your faith. Which one did you use? What worked well, and what didn't?

4. When she shared her faith with Dominic, Alex recognized a providential opening and seized the opportunity. What is a providential opening? What does it mean to seize the opportunity?

5. An easy way to initiate a Gospel presentation with an individual in the Red Zone is to say: "Someone showed me a simple diagram that reveals how someone can get closer to God. May I show it to you?" Could you see yourself using this approach? Why or why not?

6. What signs indicate a Christian is pushing too hard for a spiritual conversation to take place? What specific things can Christians do to preserve future opportunities?

7. Share a recent story you've heard of someone coming to faith in Christ. Describe how thrilling it would be (or has been) for you to help someone move from the spiritual Red Zone across the line of faith?

4

Fielding Questions

When the Washington Redskins faced the opposition, they made sure they were ready. Their coach, Joe Gibbs, said:

> We coaches would spend dozens of hours working through plays and on-field scenarios. We'd watch the films, study the stats, and scrutinize the opposing players for strengths and weaknesses, matching them to our own. In short, we'd develop a specific game plan to win that game. (*Game Plan for Life*, p. 6)

The more well-prepared their team, the more effective they became at moving the chains and getting the ball across the goal line.

RZE uses a similar strategy. Satan doesn't easily let individuals pass into God's kingdom. The spiritual forces of darkness execute a variety of plays to keep individuals away from the goal line. When Christians understand those tactics, they can be prepared to keep conversations heading in the right direction.

Internal Questions

Linda had loved Jesus for years and depended on Him to guide her day by day. She studied the Bible regularly and loved discussing spiritual matters, even with strangers. But, she rarely addressed the specifics of receiving Christ with unsaved friends, because she doubted her ability.

Too many times she'd participated in conversations that seemed to go in circles. Such interactions had undermined Linda's confidence and convinced her that evangelism wasn't her gift.

But once Linda learned the Bridge diagram, those excuses began to evaporate. Now, she knew how to help a seeker make spiritual progress. But one internal fear still held her back. What if someone asked questions she couldn't answer?

Linda's real challenge wasn't the potential of difficult questions. It was the need to face her own feelings of inadequacy and learn a powerful way to respond. Approaching her concerns from a biblical perspective provided insight.

Biblical Coaching Sessions

It's okay to feel inadequate. In fact, that may even be a good thing. At times, the Apostle Paul felt that way. In 1 Corinthians 2:3–5 he said,

> I came to you in weakness and fear, and with much trembling. My message and my preaching were not with wise and persuasive words, but with a demonstration of the Spirit's power, so that your faith might not rest on men's wisdom, but on God's power.

Paul acknowledged his inability, but trusted in God's competence instead.

Perhaps he learned that from other Apostles. When preparing them for dealing with ardent skeptics, Jesus encouraged His followers not to "worry about how you will defend yourselves or what you will say, for the Holy Spirit will teach you at that time what you should say" (Luke 12:11b–12).

Whitney Hopler, a contributing writer on Crosswalk.com, explained this practical application gleaned from Norman Geisler and David Geisler's book *Conversational Evangelism*:

> Remember that it's the Holy Spirit who ultimately draws people to Christ. You shouldn't feel the pressure of being responsible for how people respond to the Gospel. Your job is simply to lead them to it and give them opportunities to respond ("How To Share Your Faith through Conversations," available from http://www.crosswalk.com/faith/spiritual-life/how-to-share-your-faith-through-conversations-11604078.html, accessed 9/1/2012).

Only Jesus is the Savior. He pursues the lost to draw them into His eternal kingdom and relationship with Himself. For years he's been drawing your mother, your best friend, that new acquaintance.

Jesus said, "No one can come to me unless the Father who sent me draws him" (John 6:44a). God is intimately involved in the act of salvation. He simply gives His people the privilege of participating in His work. The Apostle Paul experienced that when he shared the good news with Lydia. "The Lord opened her heart to respond to Paul's message" (Acts 16:14b). Lydia was in the Red Zone.

Jerry Root, the Associate Director for the Billy Graham Institute for Strategic Evangelism and Director of Wheaton Evangelism Institute and his coauthor Stan Guthrie, an editor-at-large for *Christianity Today*, said,

> The sacramental evangelist needs to grasp the double-edged
> fact that not only is the Creator of the universe with us in our
> halting efforts to spread His good news, but He is also already
> with the other person whom we want to bless. And if God is
> already with us and our friend, doesn't it make perfect sense
> to tap into His continuing presence and power through prayer.
> (*The Sacrament of Evangelism*, p. 36)

God's power transforms the hearts of individuals. But He releases that influence through His people. In Matthew 10:19–20 Jesus said, "at that time you will be given what to say, for it will not be you speaking, but the Spirit of your Father speaking through you." Christians who develop intimacy with God and rely on Him can be confident that He will empower them to say the right thing at the right time.

But, what if a friend, relative, or acquaintance asks questions you don't know how to answer?

External Questions

God doesn't call His followers to be salespeople. He doesn't use the high-pressure techniques of today's society. Nor has He called believers to be defense attorneys. The Lord simply wants His children to testify to the reasons for the hope within them.

In all a believer's interactions, God wants her to demonstrate the fruit of the Holy Spirit—"love, joy, peace, patience, kindness, goodness, faithfulness, gentleness and self-control" (Galatians 5:22–23). These qualities can entice seekers to want the same characteristics in their own lives.

Understanding that you don't have to know how to answer every question a person asks takes the pressure off and makes it far easier to demonstrate these attributes. Learning how to deal with questions from seekers keeps believers from stressing out over what to say.

In my experience, these questions typically fall into three categories:

- Clarification

- Derailing

- Difficult

Simple solutions for each classification equip believers to handle these types of questions with confidence.

Clarification Questions

Sometimes a person will be concerned about something during the presentation of the Bridge diagram. Though an individual may express their concerns in the form of a statement, that person is actually asking an underlying question. The most common clarification questions are generally expressed with statements such as: "It seems too simple," "I'm not worthy," and "I'm already on the right side of the gap." What the person really wants to know is: "Isn't this too easy?" "Don't my failures disqualify me?" Or "I'm already on the right side of the gap, aren't I?"

Isn't this too easy? Amy had been fairly confident that Rachel was in the Red Zone. She'd asked questions about Amy's Bible study and said she was thinking of joining one at a nearby church. So Amy started praying for an opportunity to talk with Rachel about a personal relationship with Jesus. A few weeks after finishing the How To Share Your Faith training, Amy set up a time to get together.

Over dinner, they made small talk. Afterward, a providential opening occurred when Rachel said she'd joined the Bible study but that she "felt like the other ladies were discussing things over her head." She confessed to leaving early because she felt uncomfortable, especially during the prayer time.

Amy could relate. "I was in that same place two years ago. I loved the music and teaching in church, but something was missing."

Then Amy asked if she might share a diagram that helped her understand what was missing.

"Yes," Rachel responded.

Amy drew the Bridge and asked Rachel if she'd like to cross over to God's side. She said, "Well, yeah! But how?" When Amy told Rachel all she needed was to say a simple prayer between her and God, Rachel was astonished. "That doesn't seem right—it sounds too easy!"

Amy said, "You're right. It's pretty simple, but God wants to reach everyone—from the very young to the very old."

When Amy offered to lead Rachel in a prayer to ask Christ to come into her life, forgive her sins, and give her the free gift of eternal life, she got choked up: "You can do that?" she asked.

Gently Amy explained that Rachel didn't need her guidance, that the prayer was just her heart talking to God's heart. But Rachel wanted help, so Amy held her hand and led her to Christ, right in her own living room!

"Rachel couldn't thank me enough," Amy said. "I told her, it was the Holy Spirit working in her life and mine that made it happen."

Amy said that was one of the best days of her life. She couldn't sleep that night because "thankfulness to God for being faithful and present and the ease in drawing the diagram all kept playing in my head. My heart overflowed with happiness for my friend."

"Before learning RZE, talking about spiritual things had been difficult," said Amy. But since she learned how to use the Bridge and respond to concerns or questions, she no longer backs away from discussing God's love. Practice has built her confidence, so that now Amy said she even initiates spiritual conversations hoping they'll lead to eternal decisions.

Amy expressed the just-right response for the concern related to the question, *"Isn't this too easy?"* When someone says *"It just seems too simple,"* the response is *"You're right. It does seem too simple.* But it needs to be because it's for everyone—for 5 year-olds and 95 year-olds. People with an I.Q. of 40 or 140. God so loved the "world," He gave His Son for everyone. The good news is that easy.

Don't my failures disqualify me? For more than a decade, Michelle had tried to reach out to her neighbor, Cindy. But each time Michelle tried to start a conversation, a tight defense completely blocked her efforts.

During that time Cindy struggled with alcohol. But when she finally started on a journey of sobriety, she asked Michelle if she could join her Bible study. Thrilled, Michelle agreed.

"One night," Michelle said, "I asked Cindy if she wanted to receive Christ. Her response was that she wasn't good enough. A couple of ladies tried to share with her that she didn't need to be 'good' to receive God's forgiveness."

Then Michelle explained the Bridge. "The diagram made clear that it's impossible for us to be worthy enough to cross over to a holy God. His standard is absolute, and we all fall short. I explained how to pray and receive Christ (John 1:10–13)."

That was exactly what Cindy needed to know. She said, "How can I say no to a God like that?"

According to Michelle, "Cindy prayed at that moment, in her own words, for God to forgive her and come into her life."

A few weeks later, the two friends sat outside talking about the night of Cindy's conversion. Cindy mentioned that she never forgot the times she'd been drunk and walking through the neighborhood. She told Michelle, "Don't think I was ever too drunk to remember those days when you would hug me, give me a kiss and say 'I love you,' and point me back home."

Totally surprised, Michelle wondered what would have happened if she had judged Cindy and mocked her as other neighbors had. Instead, by the power of the Holy Spirit, she'd loved and valued her neighbor. Michelle said, "Joy fills my heart to know that all is in God's timing and a once lost soul is now going to spend eternity with Jesus!"

Michelle said that RZE gave her a wonderful, easy, and nonthreatening way to share the Gospel. It taught her an appropriate response for when someone expresses the concern related to the question, *"Don't my failures disqualify me?"*

When Cindy said, *"I'm not worthy,"* Michelle said: *"You're right; you're not.* Neither am I. No one is. God's standard is absolute holiness. All of us have sinned; all of us have fallen short. All of us are headed for hell. But God doesn't want anyone to go there. That's why Jesus died on the cross and rose from the dead; so you can cross over and have a relationship with God."

I'm already on the right side of the gap, aren't I? When Fiorella came into the Information Center after church, she'd been separated from God for a long time. As I asked questions, she revealed that she was angry with God because her mom was dying of cancer. I explained how God's heart is full of compassion and lovingkindness toward us. Psalm 103:11 says, "For as high as the heavens are above the earth, so great is his love for those who fear him." He does not zap people with disease and death. Instead He is "the Father of compassion and the God of all comfort, who comforts us in all our troubles" (2 Corinthians 1:3b–4a).

After awhile, Fiorella said she wanted to give her life to Christ. Evidently she'd been through the motions before, but her heart had not been right. I asked if she wanted me to pray and prompt her in what to say.

She did. So I started to pray and suggested she thank God for reaching out to her all these years. With that Fiorella began pouring out her heart to God, and the tears flowed.

Later Fiorella asked me to lead her extended family in a Bible study and share the Bridge diagram with them. Most of them had attended church growing up and thought they were on the right side of the gap, but they were relying on their church background instead of a personal connection to God.

About eighteen people gathered in the family home that Friday night. After talking about Fiorella's mom and her faith—I explained that she knew she was going to heaven and her greatest concern was to know that her family would be joining her.

I drew the Bridge diagram on a dry-erase board to show them how their church background and good works couldn't earn them a place in heaven. "God's absolute holiness requires perfection," I said. "But Romans 3:20 says, 'No one will be declared righteous in his sight by observing the law.' Every single individual falls short. Each person struggles with being self-centered instead of being dependent on God."

All people struggle with sin whether it's impatience, anger, greed, or lust, I explained. That's why Christ died in our place paying the penalty for our sins. By His resurrection He conquered death and could offer forgiveness and eternal life as a free gift. The only way to cross over the Bridge and know for certain a person is going to heaven is to receive Christ and His offer of forgiveness. Seeing the diagram helped Fiorella's extended family understand, and thirteen of them crossed over into a right relationship with their Creator.

When someone says, *"I'm on the right side of the Bridge diagram,"* a good response is to ask, *"When and how did it happen?"* If that individual says he has received Christ, be glad.

But, if his answer is unclear (for example: "I've always believed"), a follow-up question can provide good information on how to proceed. "If you die tonight and God asks, 'Why should I let you into My heaven?' what would you say?"

Responses along the lines of "Jesus died for my sins and I have received Him," necessitate nothing more than "That's great. I'm so happy to know that."

However, if someone says, "I'm a good person or I've done a lot of good things," it means he's trusting his own ability to get into heaven. Review the Bridge and explain that no one can cross over by good works.

Derailing Questions

Another type of question that comes up during the Bridge presentation can intercept the discussion at a critical point. Being strategic can prevent that from happening.

Someone might interrupt the drawing of the Bridge diagram with a difficult question right when a key point is being made. Just when the presenter starts to say, "Jesus' death on the cross paid for our sins," a seeker may blurt: "Yeah, but I don't understand why bad things happen to good people. Why does God allow tornados, earthquakes, and tsunamis to kill innocent children?" Or "What about those who have never heard this before? How can God send them to hell?"

Whatever the question might be, in the middle of the Bridge presentation is not the best time to deal with it. While drawing the diagram, if at all possible, it's best to stay focused. The seeker's response to the three concluding questions—Does this make sense?, Where are you?, and Would you like to cross over?—will determine his eternal destiny. Care must be taken at this point not to fumble for words. A good response will *affirm and postpone* the derailing question that comes during a presentation of the diagram.

When Christina presented the Bridge diagram to Sandra, she asked why a good God would allow a travesty like the Holocaust. Christina remembered to *affirm and postpone the question* and said: "That's a good question. Let's complete this diagram, and we can talk about that later."

Difficult Questions

The same questions that can derail a presentation can be tough to answer whenever they're asked. Figuring out what to say can be a challenge. But keeping it simple makes a response much easier. Either *affirm and reply* or *affirm and testify* is a satisfying way to respond.

Affirm and reply. Kevin used this method when Robert questioned "Why would an all-powerful, all-loving God let people go to hell?"

A smart guy, Kevin still didn't have a clue what to say. In fact, he kind of wondered the same thing. So he said: "That's a good question. I don't know the answer, but I'm sure there is one and I'd like to find out, too. Let me do some research and get back to you."

Kevin affirmed the question and offered to do the necessary work to find an adequate response. Following through was crucial to building trust so Kevin talked with several people and thought about the issue for himself. Then he contacted Robert to share the information. Robert appreciated Kevin's effort and the interaction continued building their relationship.

Affirm and testify. When Allison's sister, Becky, asked "Why would God let Mom get breast cancer?" Allison couldn't think of a satisfying response. But she trusted God had His reasons, so she said: "That's a good question, and sometimes I struggle with it too. I don't know the answer, but I do know that Christ is real and changed my life for the better."

Allison explained how Jesus replaced her feelings of inadequacy with more confidence. His forgiveness took away her shame and guilt. He exchanged her anxiety for peace. "Most of all," said Allison, "I feel very loved by God, and that's helped me feel good about myself and taught me to love others. There are a lot of tough questions I'll probably never be able to answer, and you probably won't either. But one thing is certain—Jesus loves us and wants a relationship with us."

The Bible describes how a blind man used a similar approach, when he boldly told hardened skeptics—I don't know the answer to that question, but "one thing I do know, I was blind, but now I see!" (John 9:25).

No one can possibly know the answer to every question, but to testify to what Jesus Christ has done in your life is powerful. Struggles with insecurity may have been replaced by confidence or fear and anxiety with God's peace. That evidence is compelling. In his book *Come Before Winter*, Chuck Swindoll explained how a person cannot argue with that kind of transformation: "The skeptic may deny your doctrine or attack your church, but he cannot honestly ignore the fact that your life has been changed" (p. 43).

Nothing to Fear

Questions can be challenging. But simple strategies can make them good tools for moving spiritual dialogue forward.

Clarification questions usually come during the presentation. The seeker is looking for understanding and needs the answer clarified. Derailing questions come up during the presentation of the Gospel, but the question can lead out of bounds, stopping the forward progress. Postponing that question keeps the presentation moving forward and provides a good opportunity for follow up later on.

Difficult questions generally arise during conversations about spiritual things. A tough question is any question for which you do not have an answer. A good response either affirms the question and promises to find the answer or affirms it, admits to not knowing, and testifies to the personal difference Christ has made. Either response will typically continue developing credibility with the person who asked.

However, in my experience, someone already in the Red Zone is far more likely to want input on how to cross the Bridge for a personal relationship with God. When I talk with a seeker, tough questions don't usually come up.

If they do, the strategies for handling clarification, derailing, and difficult questions can actually draw an individual closer to the goal. But what if they don't? What if someone in the Red Zone sees the Bridge diagram, but then says he isn't ready to cross over? That's the topic of chapter 5.

Discussion Questions

1. This chapter begins with a warning: "The evil one doesn't easily let individuals pass into God's kingdom. The spiritual forces of darkness execute a variety of plays to keep individuals away from the goal line." What moves does Satan use to prevent spiritual seekers from making progress?

2. Even after learning the Bridge illustration, an internal fear about sharing your faith may remain: What if someone asks a question you can't answer? How do you usually respond to questions you can't answer from non-Christians?

3. Jesus encouraged His followers not to "worry about how you will defend yourselves or what you will say, for the Holy Spirit will teach you at that time what you should say" (Luke 12:11b–12). Discuss reasons why you can trust God's competence when you're asked tough questions.

4. Kent suggests that tough questions from non-Christians typically fall into three categories: Clarification, Derailing, and Difficult. Define these categories, and describe their differences.

5. Define three responses to clarification questions. How do they help you?

6. What ideas do you have for doing the work necessary to find adequate responses to difficult questions?

7. In *Come Before Winter* Chuck Swindoll said, "The skeptic may deny your doctrine or attack your church, but he cannot honestly ignore the fact that your life has been changed" (p. 43). Explain the meaning of this quote.

5

Avoiding Penalties

Football coaches are constantly thinking about how to keep gaining ground and get that first down. They spend hours strategizing the best plays for certain situations—short yardage, third down, and so on. But sometimes the ball carrier runs into such strong resistance that it stops his forward progress, and the referee blows the whistle to end the play. If the ball carrier keeps pushing at that point, he may receive a penalty.

Being overeager in outreach can also place a believer at a disadvantage. A seeker may be open to seeing the "Bridge" diagram and even recognize that he is on the left side of the divide in his relationship with Christ. Yet that's when spiritual opposition intensifies. Despite the best intentions of a Christian trying to share his faith, resistance may prevent a person from being ready to cross over the line of faith. Trying to force it could damage the relationship.

Stopped at the 10-Yard Line

Misperceptions, a difficult history, or a legitimate desire to think through the issues can all keep a person from being ready to enter into a personal relationship with the Lord. Reacting too quickly could shut down a conversation instead of moving it forward. Discovering what to say in those situations helps a seeker gain important spiritual ground.

Hitting the Showers

No football player cleans up to take a shower. After a rough game, it's stepping into that overhead spray that washes him clean. To think otherwise would be considered odd. Yet, many seekers have a similar misconception.

Sometimes unsaved friends mistakenly think they have to "clean up" their lives to come to Jesus. They need to understand that coming to Jesus is like taking a shower. No one washes ahead of time. Instead, people take a shower to scrub off the dirt.

In the same way, an individual does not have to clean up his life before coming to Christ. Jesus invites each individual into a relationship just as he is. When people respond, He forgives all their sins and washes them clean from the inside. The Bridge diagram shows how that works.

Once a person has a relationship with Christ, Jesus washes that individual clean on the inside. Titus 3:4–6 explains,

> When the kindness and love of God our Savior appeared,
> he saved us, not because of righteous things we had done,
> but because of his mercy. He saved us through the washing
> of rebirth and renewal by the Holy Spirit, whom He poured
> out on us generously through Jesus Christ our Savior.

Good works won't save anyone. It's when individuals step into a union with Christ that He washes the alcoholic/prostitute/homosexual/dishonest person clean, forgives all their sins, comes into their lives and begins to transform them from the inside out—helping them become new, healthy, and whole individuals.

Getting Past Blockers

For many people, this free gift of God's grace is difficult to fathom. Some individuals have deeply entrenched spiritual obstacles.

These barriers can create such strong defenses that it may be hard to figure out where an individual is on his spiritual journey. Trying to ask for that clarity might confuse the issues. Many people wouldn't even know how to respond. But one nonthreatening question that easily engages someone in a strategic conversation is "What's your church background?"

This question relates to Christianity without being quite so direct. It side-steps all the issues related to other religions and puts the focus on Christ.

When Pete asked a fairly new friend this get-to-know-you better question, Nick said, "My background was completely secular. Neither my father nor mother wanted to influence me in a religious sense." That led to a brief dialogue where Pete expressed his belief in Christianity and appreciation for the truths it had taught him. But the guys were at a baseball game and a triple interrupted their conversation.

A couple of weeks later, while eating a fast-food hamburger, the topic of Christianity came up and Pete suggested that he could show Nick how to have a personal relationship with God. Nick shifted in his chair, crossed his arms, and looked away. Then, he started talking about something else. Pete wisely listened, following the conversation where it led.

It Takes a Team

That occasion wasn't the right timing to go further. Pete recognized that Nick was not in the Red Zone. Because they lived in different cities, they didn't really have many opportunities to connect. Fortunately Pete recognized he is only one member of a spiritual team at work in Nick's life. As a result, whenever Nick comes to mind, Pete prays that others might influence his spiritual progress.

In football, it takes eleven players to get the ball across the goal line. It's not a solo activity. The coach coordinates every player to accomplish his objective. That's true in RZE as well. No one works in isolation.

Our heavenly Coach uses many individuals and influences to draw a seeker across the line of faith. Perhaps you'll be the first to initiate a conversation, causing someone to start thinking about God in a fresh new way. Or maybe that individual will simply watch your life and admire the way your actions match your words.

The immediate objective is to keep encouraging a nonbelieving friend to make spiritual progress. Eventually, others may explain the good news to him and help him cross the line of faith. That process should never be discouraging; each step is a source of real joy for the entire body of Christ.

Hopler's article elaborated on how Geisler and Geisler describe this process in *Conversational Evangelism*:

> Sharing your faith is a process that's best done gradually through a series of conversations with people, building trusting relationships with them over time. Evangelism is helping your non-believing friends take one step closer to Christ every day and in every way. Try to make the most of every encounter with your non-believing friends to help them take steps toward Christ. ("How to Share Your Faith through Conversations," available from http://www.crosswalk.com/faith/spiritual-life/how-to-share-your-faith-through-conversations-11604078.html, accessed 9/1/2012)

An encounter with a server at a coffee shop shows how God frequently uses a team to meet people right where they are.

A Difficult Background

Monica worked at Corkey's, a restaurant I go to frequently. One slow day, I asked how she liked her job. She confided that it was important because her husband was out of work, and they had three kids. To find out how she coped with stress, I asked if she prayed.

"Not in the last five years," she said.

When I asked about her church background, she said she used to go, but hadn't done that in the past five years either. I wanted to know what happened.

After some encouragement, Monica finally responded—her voice so choked with emotion, she could barely speak the words. "My baby died in my arms."

Monica blamed God for her baby's death. Listening and caring about her pain gave me the opportunity to help her understand that Jesus hadn't abandoned her. Rather he loved her and wanted to help with her grief.

A few days later, we met at church where she could talk more freely. Monica said she'd tried to be strong because her husband and kids were "falling apart." For the first time, she poured her heart out. After she finished, I explained how the loss of her baby broke God's heart also. He doesn't rip babies out of their mother's arms. Instead, He is the God of all comfort, the Father of all mercy, and the healer of broken hearts.

"His desire is to heal your broken heart," I said. "But you have an enemy and Satan's goal is to get you to blame God for your pain and turn away from Him. By doing that you're turning away from the only One who can heal your heart and rebuild your life."

Monica wanted God's healing and committed her life to Christ that day. I gave her several verses to help her in the healing process and suggested she find a church in her area that could help her (and her family) begin to experience God and start growing in their relationship with Christ.

About a week later, I went back to Corkey's. It was Monica's day off, but a couple of other servers told me an amazing story. Evidently Monica had tripped at home and badly injured her knee. The doctor said it wasn't broken, but she needed to stay off it for several weeks.

However, her family had to pay the bills so, despite struggling with the pain, Monica went back to work. The next day, two believers dining in the restaurant asked about her limp. She told them the story, and they asked if they could pray for her. Monica said yes so they prayed right then.

According to the other servers, Monica said her knee immediately felt warm. It continued that way the rest of the day. That night she walked around the house without pain. The next day at work, she could not stop telling others about the experience.

Monica and I reconnected a few weeks later. She was so excited. Though God doesn't always heal in such a dramatic way, her pain had not returned. Plus when she had visited a church near her home she discovered that the pastor was a former high school friend. She loved his preaching, and her entire family found a church home.

I don't see Monica much anymore because the owners opened another restaurant close to her home. That seemed to be another smile from God. Her travel is much shorter, less expensive, and gives her more time with her children.

Exercising Restraint

When someone hesitates to engage in a spiritual conversation, there may be good reasons why. Losing a child, sexual abuse at the hands of a so-called spiritual figure, poor treatment by other Christians, and numerous others scenarios can build barriers to faith. It's crucial for Christians to ask questions and listen to a person's responses without becoming pushy, threatened, or defensive.

An individual's salvation is not about you. It's about the work God wants to do in that person's heart. As a believer reflects Christ's love and trustworthiness, that person may start to see Jesus and want to know more about Him.

Christians need to be engaging, not encroaching where they can unintentionally push an individual away from Christ. Honoring the person's level of interest increases sensitivity to God's providential openings for spiritual conversations and develops trust that continues to build the relationship.

Eventually an individual may become ready to see the Bridge diagram. Being conscious of the Holy Spirit's guidance, you'll know when it's appropriate to share. Even then, though, you may need to go slow and settle for the gain of only a spiritual yard or two at a time.

That's what happened when I shared the Bridge with a fireman.

Though Ron agreed to see the diagram of how to have a relationship with God, when I asked if he wanted to "cross over," he hesitated and said he wanted to think about it. Someone in the Bible did that. Following Christ's example gave me the next strategic move.

Biblical Coaching Sessions

John 3 describes how Nicodemus came to see Jesus at night. This Jewish ruler was not yet in the Red Zone, but he did have some questions. Jesus talked to Nicodemus and gave him some spiritual truths to think about. When he left Jesus, Nicodemus still had not come to the point of belief, but he was closer to the goal.

Jesus used that nighttime conversation to make spiritual progress. His response honored Nicodemus and gave him the freedom to continue processing God's word. As a result, this Pharisee eventually came to faith in Christ.

A "TAP" on the Shoulder

When my fireman friend, Ron, hesitated to receive Christ, the acronym T-A-P gave me a powerful way to help him keep moving forward on his spiritual journey.

I responded in much the same way a parent might to a daughter who needs to decide what college to attend—or perhaps a high school football coach to a budding star who's been offered several scholarships—they might tap that young person on the shoulder and say, "That's okay. To make the best possible decision, you should think about it."

A gentle touch communicates acceptance to all ages and the assurance that it's good to weigh out the facts, get questions answered, and seriously consider this life-altering choice.

The memory handle **TAP** is a good reminder of how to communicate this attitude.

- That's fine; this is between you and God.

- Any time—you can do this on your own.

- Pray. You just pray a simple prayer from your heart to God's heart if and when you're ready.

This response took so much pressure off of Ron that it led to additional dialogue and created just the opening he needed to move right into a relationship with Jesus.

Chapter 6 shows what to say when all the obstacles have been overcome and someone is ready to enter into a personal relationship with Jesus.

Discussion Questions

1. What are some examples of reacting too quickly in a spiritual conversation, being too eager, and/or trying to force things?

2. Sometimes unsaved friends mistakenly think they have to "clean up" their lives to come to Jesus. What are some good ideas for addressing this concern?

3. Why is the question "What's your church background?" non-threatening? What are some advantages of asking it? Describe someone you know who you might ask this question sometime this week.

4. Our heavenly Coach uses many individuals and influences to draw a seeker across the line of faith. What's your reaction to this "team" approach in evangelism? How does this perspective take the pressure off believers?

5. Explain in your own words the benefits of honoring a person's level of spiritual interest. Give examples of how you might do that.

6. What steps can you take to be more conscious of the Holy Spirit's guidance in gaining spiritual ground?

7. What does T.A.P. stand for and what are the advantages of using this acronym with non-Christians?

6

Going for the Goal

ouchdown! Fans jump to their feet, pump their fists in the air, and cheer. Players bump chests. Coaches smile. Everybody celebrates when someone on their team reaches the end zone.

A far greater celebration takes place whenever an individual accepts Jesus Christ as his or her Savior and Lord. Each spiritual victory fills God's heart with such gladness that even the angels rejoice. All an individual must do to cross the line of faith is express his belief in Jesus (Acts 16:31). To do so a person usually prays from his heart to God's heart, asking for forgiveness and inviting Jesus to come into his life.

Most people seeking God aren't sure how to pray and receive Christ. And, for many believers, trying to figure out how to offer assistance might seem like an overwhelming challenge.

Scripture offers God's perspective.

Biblical Coaching Sessions

The Gospel of John was written so people would "believe that Jesus is the Christ, the Son of God, and that by believing [they would] have life in his name" (John 20:30–31). The book of John uses the term "believe" or "faith" 98 times. John makes it clear again and again, that eternal life is the gift of God through faith in Christ plus nothing. Sometimes genuine faith in Christ springs from one's heart without being expressed in prayer. This appears true for Cornelius and his family. They believed in their hearts immediately as Peter explained the gospel (Acts 10:43–48). But more often people express their faith in Christ as they turn to God in prayer.

Several times Scripture uses the term "repentance," which means to change one's mind about something. Paul said "I have declared to both Jews and Greeks that they must turn to God in repentance and have faith in our Lord Jesus" (Acts 20:21; cf. 11:21). To trust Christ as Savior means someone has "changed his mind" about himself, his sin, and the Savior. He no longer trusts in his good works to get to heaven. He trusts in Christ alone (Hebrews 6:1). Repentance describes the transformation taking place in a person's heart and mind when he receives Christ as his Savior. Stories about a prodigal son, a tax collector, and a thief demonstrate.

The Prodigal Son

As this young man came to his senses and turned away from a rebellious lifestyle, he began to appreciate the importance of a relationship with his father. So, he went home to ask for forgiveness. From "a long way off, his father saw him and was filled with compassion for him; he ran to his son, threw his arms around him and kissed him. The son said to him, 'Father, I have sinned against heaven and against you'" (Luke 15:20–24).

Before a single word had been spoken, the father demonstrated acceptance. Simply by his son's turning toward home, the father understood the young man's change of heart. Though it was important for the son to confess his wrongdoing, Scripture shows no discussion. The father was already moving forward with plans for a party to celebrate. His son had come home. That's all his dad needed to know.

The Tax Collector

When the tax collector went into the temple to pray, he felt so ashamed about the things he'd done that he turned to the Lord and said, "God, have mercy on me, a sinner" (Luke 18:13).

Jesus stated that this man "went home justified before God" (Luke 18:14). A simple sincere prayer from a sinner's heart changed his eternal destiny.

The Thief

The thief on the cross did not figure out that Jesus was the Christ until the final moments of his life. Right before he died, the thief turned to the Savior and said, "Jesus, remember me when you come into your kingdom" (Luke 23:42).

This weak appeal for mercy included an unspoken request for forgiveness and grace. The thief had asked the best way he knew how.

Jesus' response was clear: "I tell you the truth, today you will be with me in paradise" (Luke 23:43). The thief received absolute assurance, a guarantee of forgiveness, and eternal life. And, Christ responds in the same way to all whose hearts humbly turn to Him (1 John 5:13).

A Spiritual Assist

Many people have recited prayers at some time in their lives but have no confidence or evidence that God heard what they said or that it made any difference. That reality makes many individuals deeply appreciate a believer's offer to guide them through a prayer helping them express their heart-felt belief in Christ as their Savior. Still, if you rarely pray out loud with another person it can feel a bit intimidating unless you look at the situation from God's perspective.

God's been reaching out to that individual for his or her entire life. Jesus wants a relationship with that person so much He died and rose again to make it possible. He has been:

- working in your brother's mind to let him know that there is a Creator, who cares about the way he lives (Romans 1:18–21).

- whispering into your sister's conscience to convict her of her need for forgiveness (Romans 2:14–16; John 16:7–11).

- knocking on your friend's heart to remind him that something is missing on the inside, something money can't buy (Revelation 3:20).

- speaking through the pressures of life to convince your coworker that she doesn't have the inner resources to cope with all that life throws at her (2 Corinthians 12:9).

- using mortality and the issue of life after death to point your new neighbor to Himself (Hebrews 9:27; Ecclesiastes 3:11).

- doing kind and loving things so that rogue relative will want to turn his life around (Jeremiah 31:3).

Once a seeker has said he'd like to cross over the "Bridge," he has recognized his need for a relationship with Jesus Christ. The Holy Spirit has already helped that person break through all the deception, confusion, pride, and stubbornness and has turned his heart to God. This individual is ready to cross the line of faith. So, what's an easy way to help take that person the rest of the way?

Russell faced this dilemma when he practiced drawing the "Bridge" diagram for his sister, Lindsey.

After attending the first session of How To Share Your Faith training, Russell was excited to share the concepts he'd learned. When Lindsey came home from college for the weekend, he asked if he might explain what it means to be a Christian. She said, "Yes."

At the following week's training, Russell shared what happened. Lindsey is deaf, so he used sign language to tell her how much God loved her and to explain the meaning of each part of the Bridge diagram. All went well until Russell finished, and Lindsey said she wanted to cross over and receive Christ. But, Russell hadn't yet learned how to help her do that. He thought it only required a simple prayer, but wouldn't learn what to say until the second session. Rather than make a mistake, Russell told Lindsey she'd have to wait.

That second week, he learned how to guide his sister through a prayer to receive Christ. Since she'd already flown back to school, Russell used a webcam and sign language to explain the next strategic move. A memorable name made it easy.

Memory Handles

To make complex strategic plays easier to remember, football teams often give them distinctive names. Each player knows exactly what to do when he hears the name of a particular play called.

In the HTSYF training, Russell also learned a simple name, **PHL**, to remind him how to explain the process of crossing the Bridge to receive Christ. To recall those letters, some people may think of a person named Phil, or perhaps the Philadelphia Eagles. These letters explain how to cross the line of faith:

- **P** = **P**ray

- **H** = **H**eart

- **L** = **L**ead

In describing this approach to Lindsey, Russell said:

"To receive Christ and enter into a personal relationship with Jesus, you simply **pray** asking God to forgive your sins and come into your life. All you do is talk from your **heart** to God's heart."

Then, he asked:

"Would you like me to **lead** you in a prayer to receive Jesus Christ right now?"

Lindsey, like most people who want to cross over the Bridge, appreciated her brother's offer to help her know what to say. Using sign language, Russell guided Lindsey through a prayer, phrase by phrase.

Another memory handle, **NFC**, helped him remember what to include. Football fans might easily recall the letters by thinking of the National Football Conference.

- **N** = **N**eed

- **F** = **F**orgive

- **C** = **C**ome

Russell prayed each phrase, then waited for Lindsey to repeat it.

"Lord Jesus, I **need** you in my life.

Please **forgive** me of all my sins.

Come into my life and lead me. Amen."

There was no need to memorize the exact words because Russell had the confidence that God would hear Lindsey's heart. When they finished, both became emotional. Russell was excited that his younger sister was the first person he'd ever led to Christ. She was thrilled to be the first individual her brother had helped into a personal relationship with Jesus.

Celebrate the Victory

Once Lindsey prayed, she crossed the line of faith and entered the eternal zone of God's kingdom. Stepping into a personal relationship with Jesus called for a celebration.

Explaining the specific benefits of what she'd done was a fantastic way to help her "spike the ball." The acronym **ESPN** reminded Russell how to explain what a relationship with Jesus means. It also helped Lindsey remember the significance of her decision to receive Christ. In the same way as he drew the Bridge diagram, Russell wrote down ESPN plus the bolded words that describe its meaning on a sheet of paper and held it up to the webcam. Then he signed the following sentence to reinforce the message. A Bible verse supplied extra value showing the relevance of Scripture.

- **E** = **E**ternal life—"Whenever you close your eyes on Earth for the last time, you'll open your eyes in God's presence in heaven." (John 6:47 says "I tell you the truth, he who believes has everlasting life.")

- **S** = **S**ins forgiven—"All your sins were forgiven, even the ones no one else knows about." (Colossians 1:14 says "in whom we have redemption, the forgiveness of sins.")

- **P** = **P**ersonal relationship—"You have begun a personal, growing friendship with Jesus Christ." (John 17:3 says "This is eternal life: that they may know you, the only true God, and Jesus Christ.)

- **N** = **N**ever leave you—You will sin again, but He will never leave you. He will be with you always. (Hebrews 13:5 says "Never will I leave you; never will I forsake you.")

Seeing those short phrases in writing reinforced God's promises in Lindsey's mind. Russell concluded their conversation by signing, "All these things happened the moment you received Christ and crossed over."

You're In

The same strategy Russell learned to lead his sister to Christ can help you with your friends, relatives, and acquaintances. Putting all the components together, you'll:

- ***Present the Bridge diagram using the key words, ask the appropriate questions, and end with the concluding question:*** "Would you like to receive Christ and cross over to the other side?" (See chapter 3.)

- ***Receive a positive response:*** "Yes, I would."

- ***Tell how to receive Christ: PHL***

   Pray—"All you have to do is say a simple prayer"

Heart—"From your heart to God's heart."

Lead—Ask, "Would you like me to lead you in a prayer to receive Jesus right now?"

- **Receive a response:**

"Yes, I would" leads to the next step. So does "No, I'd rather do it later," only rather than praying, you explain the process for how to pray and what will happen when he does (ESPN).

- **Pray and receive Christ: NFC**

"Great, let's pray. Just follow me phrase by phrase."

"Lord Jesus, I **need** you.
Forgive me for all I have done.
Come into my life and lead me."
"I pray this as sincerely as I know how, Amen."

- **Celebrate the spiritual victory with ESPN.**

You received **eternal life**.
Your **sins** have been forgiven.
You began a **personal relationship** with God.
"He will **never leave** you."

Learning what to say and practicing it quickly builds enough confidence to make you effective at assisting someone into a relationship with Jesus Christ. And, you may be surprised at the profound difference that can make in an individual's life. I'll never forget the difference it made in Mike's.

Only Believe

One afternoon I led Mike through the prayer to receive Christ. When he repeated the phrase, "God, I need you!" he broke down and cried. He finally recovered, and we continued with our short prayer. Later, I discovered that Mike had written a suicide letter that very morning. He'd intended to use his gun to take his life that same night. Sometimes I wonder what might have happened if we hadn't taken the time to talk.

Or, what if Mike had only said, "Forgive me"? What if he hadn't followed through by asking Jesus to come into his life? Would he still be saved?

Yes. Absolutely. Even when someone despairs of life, God sees the attitude of a person's heart—the words aren't the issue. Christ hears the believing heart. No one ever needs to get nervous about the specific words said in a prayer.

The key term for a relationship with Jesus in the Bible is the word "believe." John 3:16 says that "God so loved the world that he gave his one and only Son, that whoever believes in him shall not perish but have eternal life."

When the Philippian jailer asked Paul and Silas, "'Sirs, what must I do to be saved?' They replied, 'Believe in the Lord Jesus, and you will be saved'" (Acts 16:30–31). Belief refers to the attitude of a responsive heart to God.

According to 1 Samuel 16:7, "Man looks on the outward appearance, but the Lord looks at the heart." A heart that turns to God in faith motivates Him to respond.

The diagram in figure 6.1 provides an overview of the process of leading someone to Christ.

Sports fans might want to remember that the Philadelphia (**PHL**) Eagles played in the **NFC** and their games were broadcast on **ESPN**.

That sentence incorporates each of the key acronyms for RZE.

This strategy made the difference of eternity for my old high school friend, Bud. When we first reconnected by phone, we walked down memory lane. But then I asked about his spiritual journey. I told Bud, "When I get to heaven, I want to know you'll be there."

He said he was a good person, and I affirmed him in that. "But," I said, "there's a better answer, may I explain it to you?"

After he said, "Yes," I shared with Bud what Christ had done for us and that He offers forgiveness, eternal life, and a personal relationship as a free gift, but he won't force it on us. We have to receive Him.

Bud said he wanted what Christ offered, so I explained that all it took was (PHL) a prayer from his heart, and if he wanted, I could lead him in it phrase by phrase. He said "yes," so we prayed (NFC) "Lord, I need you. Please forgive my sins and come into my life and lead me." Bud received Christ right then on the phone.

Afterward, I explained ESPN, so Bud would understand the significance of what had just taken place. Bud had a terminal disease that made controlling his emotions difficult. So I asked "yes" or "no" questions to make sure he understood.

"Bud, when you die, are you going to heaven?"

"Yes," he said.

"Is it based on your good life and good works?"

"No."

"Will Christ ever leave you?"

Again, Bud said "no."

Figure 6.1. The Sandwich Principle for Receiving Christ. The three parts of the sandwich principle are stated at the bottom of the diagram. First you tell how, **PHL** (bread), then you pray, **NFC** (meat), then you tell what happened, **ESPN** (bread). The three circles on the diagram relate to each of these three parts of the process. The circled guy on the left reminds you to *tell how to receive Christ*. The circled arrow represents crossing over—reminding you to *pray and lead the seeker to Christ*. The circled guy on the right becomes God's child and reminds you to *tell him what just happened.*

He got it. His understanding of ESPN left no doubt for either of us about what had taken place. For the remainder of his life, Bud felt secure in God's love. And, what joy for me to know, my old friend will be reunited with me in heaven.

In the Here and Now

Besides giving eternal security, ESPN makes new believers more aware of God's love and creates the desire to know Jesus better, trust Him more, and follow Him day by day. Motivation to live for Jesus comes from understanding who He is and what He has done. So it's important for new believers to appreciate Christ's sacrifice on the cross. "We love because he first loved us" (1 John 4:19).

Now that the basic strategy for RZE has been laid out, some extra training tips can make it even more winsome. Chapter 7 explains the importance of practice.

Discussion Questions

1. Why is it so difficult for believers to explain to a seeker how to pray, ask for Christ's forgiveness, and invite Him into her life? Is this something you've ever done with a non-Christian? If so, describe what happened.

2. How does the reality that many individuals deeply appreciate a Christian's offer to guide them through such a prayer motivate you to learn how to assist them?

3. Once an individual recognizes his need for a relationship with Jesus Christ, PHL is an easy way to help that person take the next step? Why should you be fully prepared for this moment?

4. What does NFC stand for and how might it be helpful? Do you have any questions or concerns about using this memory handle, and if so what are they?

5. Describe ways you could celebrate the life-changing decision of a new believer to enter into a personal relationship with Jesus.

6. What does the acronym ESPN stand for, and why is it important to reinforce God's promises to a new believer soon after he or she receives Christ?

7. If God sees a person's heart, how important is it for a person to actually say "the prayer?" Do the words make a difference? Give reasons for your response.

7

Improving the Odds

Chuck Noll, head coach for the Pittsburgh Steelers from 1969–1991, won four Super Bowl championships in a six-year period. Noll led the Steelers to a winning record in 15 of his last 20 seasons with the team.

When it came to practicing the fundamentals and paying attention to the details, Noll said, "Champions are champions not because they do anything extraordinary but because they do the ordinary things better than anyone else." (*Quiet Strength* by Tony Dungy, p. 105)

John Wooden—the legendary coach of UCLA's record-setting basketball team—would agree. His insistence on preparation led those he coached to extraordinary results. They won 10 national championships in 12 years. Wooden's value for strategic planning explains this phenomenal success:

> The time to prepare isn't after you have been given the opportunity. It's long before that opportunity arises. Once the opportunity arrives, it's too late to prepare. (*A Lifetime of Observations and Reflections on and off the Court* by John Wooden and Steve Jamison, p. 130)

Wooden's legacy has impacted coaches of all sorts, including myself. Whether drilling athletic teams, instructing the leadership of organizations, or preparing people for outreach in the Red Zone—advance planning and practice builds confidence and makes people more effective. Wooden describes the preparation process:

> The four laws of learning are explanation, demonstration, imitation, and repetition. The goal is to create a correct habit that can be produced instinctively under great pressure. To make sure this goal was achieved, I created eight laws of learning; namely, explanation, demonstration, imitation, repetition, repetition, repetition, repetition, and repetition. (*A Lifetime of Observations*, p. 144)

These laws are just as effective for Christians as they are for anyone. Plus for believers, they hold eternal value. The Bridge diagram—using memorable key words, questions, and phrases (see chapters 3 and 4)—provides the explanation. My experiences demonstrate how this outreach approach works as does the experiences of others who have used it. But what makes RZE so effective is repetition until it becomes instinctive.

A dramatic life-and-death crisis shows the value of practicing this method until it becomes a habit.

Practice Banishes Fear

One day Angela, a friend from church, asked me to go to the hospital to visit her elderly father who had suffered a massive stroke. While connected to life-support equipment, additional strokes had destroyed Manuel's entire respiratory system as well as other organs. Angela hoped I could lead her father to Christ before he died.

When I arrived at the hospital, Manuel was heavily medicated. Doctors intended to rouse him for a few minutes so the family could say their last good-byes. At that time, I'd explain salvation to him. Afterward, when the family was ready, he'd be put back under heavy sedation while doctors weaned him off life-support. Then he'd enter eternity—either for judgment or everlasting life.

As the doctors awakened Manuel, the family talked with him to make sure he was conscious and could understand. Then they introduced me as their pastor.

A large tube in his airway helped him breathe, so he could not speak. But he could move his eyes and his head, just barely.

I told Manuel how much his family loved him. Their greatest concern was to know that when they got to heaven, he'd be there.

For the next several moments, I described how God loved him and wanted a personal relationship, but that selfishness and sin created a deep gulf between each individual and God. All our attempts to breach that divide result in death—spiritual and physical. None of our good works can save us.

Manuel's deep brown eyes never left my face as I began to describe how Christ died to pay the penalty for our sins. His resurrection permitted Jesus to freely offer us forgiveness and eternal life with Him. Yet God won't force salvation on us. He waits for us to ask His forgiveness and invite Him into our lives.

At that point, I asked Manuel if he'd like me to lead him in a simple prayer between his heart and God's. His answer would determine his eternal destiny.

Manuel's daughter breathed a sigh of relief as her father nodded "yes." Tears streaked his wrinkled face as he closed his eyes to pray. When we finished, I explained what God had promised him by going over ESPN—eternal life, all his sins forgiven, a personal relationship with Jesus and that He would never leave.

Then I backed away from the bed so the family could gather close, love on him, and say their final good-byes.

Angela and her family certainly grieved the loss of Manuel, but they had the joy of knowing he was with Jesus. Because Manuel crossed the goal line of his spiritual journey, their separation would only be temporary. Eventually, they'd all be together again, forever.

Despite having shared my faith with several terminally ill patients, knowing there are only a few minutes to present the Gospel can produce a heart-pounding situation. In a crisis, it's crucial to know what to say to move the conversation from point A to point B. Rehearsing and repeating the Bridge diagram presentation along with the acronyms, again and again has made them so instinctive that I can easily carry the dialogue in the right direction without fear.

Can you? What if your mother, brother, friend, or acquaintance has but a few minutes before eternity, and our heavenly Coach designates you to assist them into His kingdom? Practice can equip you to carry a spiritual conversation even during the most dire circumstances. With earthquakes, tornadoes, and blizzards—potential terrorism, car accidents, and disease—God can call on anyone at anytime to share his faith. And, it might not even be a life-or-death situation that instigates the challenge.

The story of an introvert shows how practice can bring about eternal victories when least expected.

Practice Builds Confidence

Eric's an accountant. He considers himself socially awkward and likes to remain behind the scenes. Though he enjoys his family and friends, Eric's not likely to walk up to strangers to say "hello." And, he has no desire to stand on the corner or go house-to-house to share his faith.

At 48-years-old, he's never done that, nor does he think he ever will.

"Giving money or time was easier as long as I didn't have to interact or carry on a conversation for more than just a few minutes," said Eric. "But this year Christ has been working in my heart telling me it's time to step up." Deciding he wanted to be ready "just in case," when the opportunity came to attend a How To Share Your Faith training, Eric signed up.

In that setting, I asked each participant to recall the key words they'd learned and use them in sentences. Eric filled in the blanks and repeated the key phrases step by step.

At the end of the training, Eric told me, "I don't see myself ever using these tools, but at least now I'm prepared."

Months later, when the phone rang and I answered it, I was surprised to hear Eric's voice. He wanted to tell me about an amazing experience.

"A coworker came into my office, obviously upset. Matt needed someone to talk to about what was happening in his life. He'd been married less than a year, but had recently separated. We were discussing this painful situation when Matt mentioned that he'd attended a couple of church services and had been doing a little reading.

That's when a dialogue started in my head. A voice whispered in my mind that this was it—the moment to use my new tool. I thought, *"Now? No, I don't think so."* Excuses flashed in my mind: *It's during work. He's a coworker. What if he rejects the whole thing? I'm not supposed to discuss religion at work. What if I mess up?*

Then, I heard that firm quiet voice, again. *"Yes, now."*

A few years earlier, Eric said he knew there had been an occasion when God wanted him to share his faith. But it turned out to be a disaster. "It did not fail because the other person rejected my message," said Eric, "but because I never started the conversation."

A month later Eric tried to recreate that opportunity, only to find out that the individual had moved away. "Upon realization that I would never be able to talk with him, God hit me with an *ah-ha* moment. My friend would be saved with or without me, but the failure was my disobedience to God. I promised Him and myself that next time would be different."

So this time Eric gave a silent "OK" to the whisper in his mind and asked his first strategic question. "What's your church background?"

Matt responded with openness and Eric breathed a sigh of relief. His coworker's honesty encouraged Eric to ask more questions: "How's your relationship with God now?" "Do you know if you're going to Heaven?"

When Matt answered that question with "No," Eric thought *oh boy, here we go*. A bit shaky, he used familiar words and did the best he knew how. "A diagram I got from a seminar kind of shows how to get there. Would you like to see it?"

"Sure," Matt responded.

Wow, textbook—just like the training, thought Eric.

So he pulled out a piece of paper and proceeded to draw the diagram using the dialogue he'd been taught—well sort of. "I was so nervous I could barely say the words, some never came out, and what did was out of order. The diagram was sloppy, messed-up, full of lines, and my penmanship was horrendous. But in the end, we got there."

Then Eric asked, "Where are you today?"

After Matt pointed to the left side of the divide, Eric asked "Would you like to cross over?"

Matt said, "Yes."

"I can help with that," replied Eric slowly, taking a moment to think about what he'd practiced and the acronyms that would help him remember the words.

"If you're ready, we can do it right now," said Eric. "It's a simple prayer from your heart to God's heart."

"Yes, I'd like that," replied Matt.

They prayed—"Lord, I need you. Please forgive my sins, and come into my life and guide me."

After the "Amen," Eric followed up with ESPN to explain the benefits of salvation—eternal life, sins forgiven, and never alone. "I got most of it," said Eric, "but never did remember what "P" represented. When we finished, my first thought, which I probably spoke out loud, was '*Wow, this stuff really works.*' I knew God was in the room because even after that fumbling presentation, Matt accepted Christ."

Later Eric said, people who knew him were surprised to hear what happened. Eric's wife thought that he might be fired for talking about religion in the workplace. The guys in his small group were utterly amazed. But the real surprise to everyone, including Eric, was that about three weeks later, it happened again.

But this time, Eric was better prepared. His initial experience, plus some additional practice, gave him a bit more confidence when a spiritually significant conversation took place with somebody he'd just met.

It happened during a sales meeting with a potential vendor. Eric described Brandon as a "kid in his early twenties, young, and energetic." In contrast Eric was struggling with lower back pains, which forced him to be stooped over.

While they were talking, Brandon said something about being eager to grow up and have all the adult experiences. Eric replied that if there was any advice he could give, it would be: "Take your time. Getting old is not all it's cracked up to be. Enjoy every day and make sure that God is in your life."

A couple more minutes of conversation passed, then Brandon asked, "Are you a Christian?"

Eric leaned back in his chair, pushed up his glasses, and replied, "Yes, how about you?" Brandon said he wasn't, but had recently been going to church with his girlfriend. He'd also been reading the Bible. They started discussing some of the questions he had about Christianity. When Brandon said he believed there's something more, Eric asked if he wanted to know how to take the step to become a Christian. Brandon said, "Yes."

It only took a few minutes for Eric to draw the Bridge diagram and explain it. He asked the three key questions—Does that make sense? Where are you? and Do you want to cross over?

After Brandon said "yes," to the last one, Eric offered to lead him in a prayer. Brandon accepted Christ right there in the conference room. And, this time when Eric explained ESPN, he even remembered that "P" stood for "personal relationship."

Later, when Eric reflected on his experiences, one factor that stood out was God's presence and guidance during the conversation. The Holy Spirit had obviously been working in the lives of those Eric had spoken with. They were definitely in the Red Zone. It was also clear that even though he had done a poor job of drawing the diagram and fumbled with his words, God had granted both seekers enough understanding that they accepted Christ.

Practice Increases Playing Time

In football, when a running back is ready, the coach gives him more "touches"—chances to carry the ball through rushing attempts, pass receptions, or kickoff returns. Within the spiritual realm, God is a believer's "Coach." When a Christian makes the effort to be prepared to assist people in the Red Zone, God seems to put him in the game more often, giving him more "touches"—chances to help seekers cross the line of faith. Eric's two "divine appointments" became a wake-up call and he began to exercise far more diligence in learning about the different nuances of outreach.

His goal? To create a habit so instinctive, it can be produced even under great pressure.

Additional training tips in chapter 8 reveal ways to make RZE all the more effective.

Discussion Questions

1. Give a definition for each of John Wooden's laws of learning. How do these laws apply to Christians attempting to become effective in sharing their faith?

2. Can repetition of the RZE approach lead to an instinctive ability (or habit) to apply the principles in everyday life? Why or why not? Describe how an instinctive reaction to an evangelistic opportunity might look.

3. Considering the story about Manuel, on a scale from 1–10, how prepared are you to present the Gospel in a compelling way during a crisis? Give reasons for the number you selected. What might improve your preparedness?

4. What's the best way for you to rehearse the Bridge diagram and when will you carve out time to practice explaining it? Consider partnering with someone to learn and rehearse this illustration or download the Bridge App from ShareYourFaithApp.com.

5. What excuses might flash across your mind to avoid sharing your faith, even though you sense God has opened a door for you? How can you build confidence, so you won't cave in and bail at opportune times?

6. Are you convinced God can use you to help bring someone across the line of faith, even if you stumble through the presentation and forget a few of the words? Why or why not? Where does God's presence and guidance fit when it comes to being effective in evangelism?

8

Moving the Chains

Every football team does all it can to move the ball forward. Each time the offense completes a play that gains a first down, the team moves the chains and edges closer to the goal. That's the objective; the team wants to get the ball across the goal line.

When believers consciously strive to behave in ways that encourage spiritual progress, they, too, keep moving the chains. In *Tell It Often, Tell It Well,* author Mark McCloskey describes how he cultivates this winning attitude by praying for two things:

> First, that God would lead me to people who are ready to decide, so that I might help them to enter His kingdom; second, that God would grant me the wisdom to determine where my listeners are in the decision-making process, so that I might speak to their point of need with relevance and with the gospel's authority. (p. 226)

Only God can bring the right words to speak to an individual's "point of need." That vulnerable place of relevance is likely so hidden that uncovering it requires the gentleness of divine insight. It takes great sensitivity to assist with drawing a seeker toward Christ. At the same time, being too hesitant to speak up could prevent a conversation from gaining new spiritual territory. Asking the Lord for His words and wisdom achieves the just-right balance at the just-right time.

A core value to keep in mind with personal outreach is to *honor the person*. Reviewing Scripture reveals some good examples.

Biblical Coaching Sessions

The Bible reveals great role models for Christians. When it comes to outreach, Philip and Peter each teach some powerful lessons.

Philip

When Philip ran up to the chariot and found a man reading Isaiah the prophet, he (Philip) didn't make assumptions (see Acts 8:30–39). Instead he asked a question to assess the situation and establish relevance. "Do you understand what you are reading?" he asked.

After the Ethiopian invited Philip's input, he didn't proceed with his own agenda but rather answered the eunuch's questions. Philip met the Ethiopian right at his place of need. Even after explaining the good news, Philip didn't tell the eunuch what he needed to do, but rather responded to his request to be baptized. Then, the Holy Spirit whisked Philip away.

Philip didn't try to impart a flood of information to the Ethiopian. Instead, Philip stayed sensitive to God's leading. When the Lord led Philip elsewhere, the eunuch remained in God's care.

Peter

Though Peter wasn't always known for being tactful, he showed great reliance on God when the Holy Spirit led him to Cornelius (see Acts 10:9–48). Even when God told Peter to give up his long-standing practices and prejudices to relate to someone who wanted a relationship with the risen Savior, Peter obeyed. Going to the Gentile's home, Peter met Cornelius in his comfort zone and asked about his needs.

Peter reminded Cornelius of what he already knew then testified about Christ's sacrifice on the cross. The Holy Spirit worked among everyone present to maximize the impact of Peter's message.

God alone can assess an individual's openness. He alone knows exactly what each person needs to hear. However, biblical insights can guide Christians in the most effective way to deliver that good news.

- "Do not let any unwholesome talk come out of your mouths, but only what is helpful for building others up according to their needs, that it may benefit those who listen" (Ephesians 4:29).

- "Be wise in the way you act toward outsiders; make the most of every opportunity. Let your conversation be always full of grace, seasoned with salt, so that you may know how to answer everyone" (Colossians 4:5–6).

- "But in your hearts set apart Christ as Lord. Always be prepared to give an answer to everyone who asks you to give the reason for the hope that you have. But do this with gentleness and respect" (1 Peter 3:15).

Believers must be careful not to come across as arrogant or as though they have all the answers. Keeping these biblical examples in mind will move dialogue in the right direction. Some additional key principles will also help.

Forward Motion

In a world hostile to Jesus Christ, the Gospel itself can be considered offensive. However, honoring a person's beliefs frequently overcomes that obstacle. Being sensitive and respecting an individual's thoughts opens up conversation. Not arguing doesn't signify agreement. Rather respectful listening makes an individual feel valued.

In his book *Seeker Small Groups: Engaging Spiritual Seekers in Life-Changing Discussions*, Garry Poole said:

> What seekers need most of all is to be listened to empathetically.... What really makes a significant impact is demonstrating an authentic, caring, and understanding heart toward seekers by the way you listen. And that is definitely something you can do! (p. 161)

Other key principles also increase spiritual momentum. A seeker will be more responsive if you:

1. Genuinely care about him.
2. Find out how open she is to God.
3. Attempt to discover below-the-surface needs.
4. Help him see his pain from a biblical perspective.
5. Pray with him, lifting him into God's presence.
6. Show her God's character and how He responds to those who love Him.
7. Suggest ideas for what God may be doing in her circumstances.

These principles add such tremendous value to relationships, they're worth exploring in more detail.

1. *Genuinely care about each individual.*

Motivators from President Theodore Roosevelt to leadership expert John Maxwell have spoken about the principle that "people don't care what you know until they know that you care." In Habit #5 of Stephen Covey's bestselling book, *The 7 Habits of Highly Effective People*, he rephrased this concept as: "seek first to understand, then to be understood" (p. 235). It's a habit worth cultivating because it works.

No matter who it might be—a new acquaintance, a relative, or a coworker—when people sense that someone genuinely cares about them and wants to hear about their lives, they are much more inclined to open their hearts to discuss spiritual matters.

Busyness, even in ministry, can easily distract Christians from being interested in the lives of those around them. Taking time and making the effort not to be so task-oriented permits believers to touch the lives of those who need to see Jesus.

God's second greatest commandment challenges Christians to love others as themselves. Seeing people through God's eyes and caring about what's important to them frequently earns believers the right to communicate the good news.

But, it may not. If a person's not in the Red Zone, then a Christian needs to be especially sensitive to that individual's level of interest and proceed with caution. Later, if he knows you care, that same person may start seeking Christ.

2. *Find out how open a person is to God*

Asking questions, listening, and responding in ways sensitive to an individual's level of spiritual openness builds relationships. In that process, Christians can assess a person's concerns about spiritual matters. Humbly giving a biblical perspective will help that individual feel valued and hear what you have to say. A Christian can't easily be faulted for saying, "I believe…" or "If I remember right, the Bible says…" Likewise, avoiding "you" statements will generally prevent people from becoming defensive. For example: "You should read the Bible," "You need to go to church," or "You should hear this sermon" can shut down a conversation fast.

Sometimes a person may be blaming God for the hard things in her life. Another individual may need understanding about how God could become a man. Someone else may want to know that Christ is real and can help in his personal circumstances, career, or relationships. Or an individual might struggle with understanding the hypocrisy she sees in the life of a Christian.

It may take several conversations before this type of information reveals itself. But the patience, love, and encouragement of a friend should move the conversation forward over time. And, remember you don't have to have all the answers.

3. Attempt to discover below-the-surface needs

Most people experience deep stress, hurt, or fear at some point in their lives that increases their openness to spiritual input. Emotional pain often puts an individual in the Red Zone.

One web site reported that "several research studies of lasting adult conversions have shown…that: for over 60% of conversions, a serious life problem played a large part in starting them on the journey" (see www.internetevangelismday.com/relationships.php, accessed 9/1/2012).

Well-known psychologist and Bible teacher Larry Crabb advises believers on how to gain insight into the situation:

> *Think beneath.* See the real battle that's being fought in someone's soul. It will require supernatural discernment to think beneath the problems people share and identify the battle going on in their soul that most folks never see…. Meet the real person you are talking with. Be curious about the story he is reluctant to tell and about the shaping events of his life, through which he learned what to value more than God. It will require supernatural listening to become a safe enough person that another will want to be explored by you. (*Soul Talk*, p. 31)

Developing trustworthy relationships is powerful. Some people don't have a single person who cares that much. Being a true friend who takes the time to ask questions and listens to their answers can move someone into a significant spiritual dialogue.

4. *Help people see their pain from God's perspective.*

Some people become locked in their pain and need spiritual insight to get past it. A recent encounter with Rick and his girlfriend illustrates.

Carla had deep hurts that kept her from a relationship with God. After Rick introduced us, I asked about her story. She described how over a two-year period she'd lost her baby, her mother, brother, uncle, niece, and best friend due to various diseases. Death had robbed Carla of the circle of people closest to her, and she couldn't understand why God allowed that to happen. Carla was angry.

I asked questions and listened to all Carla had to say. Then, I explained that God had created Adam and Eve and given them life. But they believed Satan's lies and chose to turn away from God. Rebelling, they ignored His authority and did things their own way. That was sin, and the result was death—spiritual and physical. Diseases that led to death became part of the human condition (see Romans 5:12).

In much the same way as Satan lied to Eve, he whispered lies into Carla's mind. The evil one convinced her she couldn't trust God, so she blamed Him for the deaths of her loved ones. Paul expressed this concern in 2 Corinthians 11:3. "But I am afraid that just as Eve was deceived by the serpent's cunning, your minds may somehow be led astray from your sincere and pure devotion to Christ."

Satan wanted to keep Carla from knowing "the Father of compassion and the God of all comfort, who comforts us in all our troubles" (2 Corinthians 1:3–4). Yet He is the only one who can heal her heart and help her cope with such intense pain and horrendous loss.

That information made sense to Carla so, with her permission, I drew out the Bridge diagram. Then I showed her how to cross over into a personal relationship with God. She prayed a beautiful, repentant, heartfelt prayer and asked Christ to forgive her anger and begin the healing process. Helping Carla see her hurts and wounds from a biblical perspective turned the key that unlocked her heart for Jesus.

5. *Pray "for" and "with" those who need the Lord.*

A Christian's most effective outreach tool is prayer. The Internet Evangelism Day website reports that:

> Several research studies of lasting adult conversions have shown… in over 70% of conversions, a relationship with a Christian(s) who subsequently turned out to be praying for them was the strongest factor—far more significant than reading the Bible, tracts, books or watching videos. They wanted what they saw modeled in their friends' lives. (See http://www.InternetEvangelismDay.com/relationships.php#ixzz1gegAgLuj, accessed 9/1/2012.)

Offering to pray for a seeker either in person or over the phone builds a relationship in fresh new ways. There's a good chance no one has ever asked to do that before. It lowers an individual's defenses and creates instant bonds.

When I see people who are struggling and wondering if God cares, I usually ask if I can pray for them. If they agree, we bow our heads, and I ask God to be merciful and intervene in their situation, to touch them, to help them experience His peace, presence, and love. Afterward, they often look up with tears in their eyes and thank me. Frequently that's the turning point in their journey toward God.

6. *Help people see God's character and how He responds to those who love Him.*

Christians are leaders who model the way for others. If they are brash, rude, defensive, or arrogant, nonbelievers may wonder why anyone would want to follow Jesus. However, when a believer reflects the fruit of the Holy Spirit—"love, peace, patience, kindness, goodness, faithfulness, gentleness and self-control" (Galatians 5:22–23)—those character traits can be so enticing, they draw someone across the line of faith and into a relationship with the Lord.

As people share their stories, listen with empathy. By seeing your heart, they'll sense God's heart and compassion. Sharing a verse of Scripture that has been meaningful to you in hard times might convince a seeker that God also cares for him.

7. *Suggest ideas for what God may be doing in a person's circumstances.*

Sometimes when I see the activity of God in an individual's experience, I'll attempt to interpret for him what God is doing.

Depending on what's happening, I might say: "It seems like God is reaching out to you," or "Maybe God is showing you He loves you," or "It looks like God might be nudging you in that direction." I try to help her recognize Christ's active involvement in the experience so she'll realize He's at work in her life.

In *Waking the Dead*, John Eldredge wrote:

> Until we come to terms with *war* as the context of our days we
> will not understand life. We will misinterpret 90 percent of what
> is happening around us and to us.
>
> …You won't understand your life, you won't see clearly what has
> happened to you or how to live forward from here, unless you
> see it as *battle*. A war against your heart….There are a few things
> I know, and one thing I do know is this: we don't see things as
> clearly as we ought to. As we *need* to. We don't understand what's
> happening around us or to us or to those we love. (p.17–18)

That's why believers, who do have spiritual insight, need to help
people understand their experience from God's perspective. With
a biblical worldview, Christians can aid seekers so they'll recognize
God's presence and grasp His purposes.

Using All 7 Keys

Reality is God's truth. By instigating spiritual discussions Christians
can help people see reality and understand their experience from
God's perspective. Looking beneath the surface uncovers past hurts
and wounds. When believers offer kindness and genuinely care, others
more easily recognize Jesus at work and reject the lies of the enemy.
That empathy encourages them to turn to God, trust Him, and respond
to His direction in their lives. When Christ's disciples pray for wisdom
and speak gentle truths into a person's life, the Holy Spirit affirms the
words and usually leads seekers forward toward healing and freedom.

This process moves the chains and may even lead to a presentation
of the "Bridge" diagram. But the spiritual journey certainly doesn't
end there. After a person receives Christ, he still needs to grow in his
faith. Chapter 9 answers the question, "What next?"

Discussion Questions

1. How does the football concept of "moving the chains" relate to making progress in evangelism? Give examples. What role does prayer play in "moving the chains?" At the conclusion of your time together, pray and ask God to move the chains in a specific person's life.

2. This chapter discusses the core value of "honoring the person" in personal outreach. How might this attitude overcome the obstacle of Christians being considered offensive?

3. Select one or two key principles that will increase spiritual momentum and explain in detail how they might add tremendous value in relationships.

4. When it comes to building relationships with non-Christians, what are "trust-builders," and what are "trust-busters?" Explain your response.

5. Is there a non-Christian in your life, who is struggling, that you could offer to pray for this week? How might that lower his defenses and create bonds between you?

9

Finishing the Game

One touchdown doesn't reveal the results of an entire game. The first time a wide receiver crosses into the end zone definitely marks a significant event, but much more takes place before the game comes to an end.

Though salvation is once-and-for-all forever, stepping from the Red Zone into God's kingdom only marks the beginning of a personal relationship with Jesus Christ. God's transformation of a new believer into the likeness of Christ continues throughout a person's lifetime. That's why believers using RZE frequently ask, "What do I do next?"

I usually suggest several valuable resources.

The Right Equipment

When an individual begins a new relationship with Jesus, I typically offer the following materials:

- *Would You Like to Know God Personally?* by Bill Bright. This 15-page booklet from New Life Publications provides an excellent review of the Gospel and the prayer to receive Christ along with several helpful verses. It contains useful information to explain what happens when an individual enters into a personal relationship with Jesus. It also provides some good suggestions for spiritual growth and describes the importance of becoming involved in a church where Christ is honored and His Word is preached.

- *Beginning with Christ* by the Navigators. This 8-page booklet, published by NavPress, uses five biblical promises to prepare new believers to respond to the common doubts the enemy typically whispers into their minds. These verses and explanations deal with the assurance of:

  1. salvation,
  2. answered prayer,
  3. victory,
  4. forgiveness, and
  5. guidance.

- *My Heart Christ's Home* by Robert Munger. This classic 28-page booklet, published by IVP Books, compares a person's life to a home and describes the process of progressively inviting Christ into different areas to clean them up and make them more functional. Dr. Munger explains how this process is directly connected to spending time alone with Christ each day, talking to Him through prayer, and listening to Him by reading and responding to His Word.

Each of these booklets is an easy read, powerful and relevant for someone who wants to grow in Christ.

It's also good to suggest that a new believer begin reading at least one chapter a day in the Gospel of John. If she does not have a contemporary copy of the Bible, I give her a paperback New Testament (with study notes for new believers), usually in the New Living Translation. BiblicaDirect.com has them available for $1.25 (see http://www.biblicadirect.com/c-53-new-living-translation-nlt.aspx). When I hand a copy to someone, I explain the layout of the notes and bookmark where the Gospel of John begins.

Because RZE focuses on building relationships, most of the time Christians already know the individuals they lead to Christ. The new believer might be a friend, a neighbor, or a relative. He could be someone at the gym, at school, a social event, or a service club meeting. She might be a business contact, a bank teller, a doctor, dentist, or repair technician.

These types of ongoing relationships include built-in follow-up possibilities, so it's not necessary to try to tell that person everything at once. When it comes to processing spiritual information, receiving a glass of water is a far more effective way to drink than trying to sip from a fire hose.

The Bible supplies additional insights for effective ways to further encourage new believers to grow in their beliefs.

Biblical Coaching Sessions

Jesus told His followers that:

> Everyone who hears these words of mine, and puts them into practice is like a wise man who built his house on the rock. The rain came down, the streams rose, and the winds blew and beat against that house; yet it did not fall, because it had its foundation on the rock. (Matthew 7:24–26)

The best place to consistently *hear* God's word and be challenged to practice it is in a healthy, vibrant church. Participation in a body of believers establishes an individual's "house" on solid biblical ground.

Vital relationships with other Christians will strengthen a new believer and help him consider ways to apply God's word to his life. Then, when life's storms come, believers will stand on the rock of Christ.

Spiritual Growth

New believers must learn how to live life based on the Coach's wisdom. Jesus wants them to become His followers and replace their own ways with His. The goal is not only to get decisions, but also to make disciples.

Finding the right church home and building a strong spiritual support system will assist new believers in scoring eternal victories in their everyday lives. Yet trying to figure out these things can be a challenge even for seasoned Christians. Some simple ideas supply a distinct advantage.

Finding the Right Church Home

If a new believer lives nearby and there's no significant resistance to attending church, an easy way to introduce him to the spiritual life is to invite him to come with you. That should ease any fears he may have about going alone. Asking him out for breakfast or lunch, either before or after the service, can provide extra incentive to accept your invitation.

Sometimes, though, you'll take a new believer to church only to discover she doesn't appreciate the same worship style you do. When that happened to Nikki, she responded in a way that changed her neighbor's life.

Nikki invited Lori to come to a Sunday service soon after she became a Christian. Lori went but the loud music and vocal praising of God made her uncomfortable, and she didn't want to go back.

Hearing about those issues, Nikki suggested a more conservative church. But it was so large, Lori felt lost. She never returned.

A few weeks later, Nikki and Lori chatted over the back fence. A single mom with a little boy, Lori confessed how lonely she was. She didn't want to go out drinking any more, but now she didn't have any friends. Nikki decided to try once more, "You really need to be in church."

"I know," said Lori, "but I didn't like the ones you took me to."

The Holy Spirit prompted Nikki to empathize. As she did, a flash of insight came. "I know one you might try," Nikki said, trying to control her enthusiasm. "It's a small church with people your age. I think you'll like it."

Lori decided to check it out and the first time she went, loved it. People were warm and friendly. There were other children her son's age and the simple worship songs ministered to her aching heart. She'd found a church home where she could grow in her relationship with Jesus.

Asking someone if he has any friends who go to church might be another good way for a new believer to connect with Christians who have common interests. Many churches hold special events that can also be a good introduction for new people who may be hesitant about going to regular services.

Developing a Godly Support System

Most new Christians are eager to belong to the body of Christ. Yet sometimes figuring out how to get to church can be a challenge. A new believer might work Sundays or be convinced he doesn't have time. Some people have had difficult church experiences and are not quite ready to go back into that environment. Or some may simply have negative perceptions about church.

That makes a positive connection to the body of Christ all the more important. By being kind and understanding, asking questions and addressing concerns, Christians can encourage new believers to get to know Jesus better. Remembering that God guides each individual's spiritual journey takes the pressure off of trying to force the situation.

Rather than setting expectations that might damage a relationship, offering a variety of options encourages new believers to grow in their relationship with Jesus.

If church isn't a viable option now, that doesn't mean it won't be in the future. In the meantime, a Bible study may be a good nonthreatening option. Weekly meetings in structured groups like Community Bible Study (see http://www.communitybiblestudy.org/) or Bible Study Fellowship (BSF, see http://www.bsfinternational.org/) teach thousands of people to study God's Word and apply it to their lives. As they develop a biblical worldview, Christians often come to the realization that they need to attend church on a regular basis. Both of these studies have solid reputations and offer classes throughout the United States and in many foreign countries.

In most of these classes, men meet with men and women with women providing good opportunities for learning from positive role models. One-on-one interaction also gives a new believer the opportunity to ask questions, learn, and grow in their faith.

A class for new Christians at a local church can be another valuable option. New believers often have similar concerns, and one individual might think of a question another one doesn't. Any interaction that encourages relationships and builds godly support with other believers will help a new believer start applying biblical principles to their lives.

It Takes a Team

No one can win a football game by themselves. Life on the spiritual playing field also requires interaction with others. Every believer needs the Lord's coaching and the involvement of other believers.

The most valuable resource of every Christian is the guidance of the Holy Spirit. Whether it's to bring someone to Christ, find a church, or develop godly support, Jesus knows how to best develop an individual's faith and connect them with the godly support system they need. So it's critical to involve Him in the process through prayer.

In addition, God uses other members in the body of Christ to assist new believers. A phone call from a college-aged pastor inviting a new young-adult believer to an event might be a spiritual turning point. Many churches have dynamic young-adult pastors who would be pleased to make that call if asked. Young moms might appreciate being invited to a Mothers of Preschoolers breakfast, even by someone they just met. A dad might be glad if a more spiritually mature man invites him to lunch just to get acquainted.

Social media can be a good tool to help connect new believers who live in a different area with other Christians. One woman in Southern California asked a Facebook friend in Las Vegas about healthy churches. That started a discussion about the various characteristics of nearby churches. As a result, her young friend found several that might suit her needs. Managers of Christian bookstores might also offer suggestions of vibrant spiritually healthy churches.

Being willing to do the research or offer suggestions to help new Christians transition from a lifestyle based on the world's values to a life filled with eternal purpose will build momentum in a new believer's spiritual life. And, that's a win for everyone involved.

To God be the Glory

For every spiritual conversion, God deserves all the glory, honor, and praise. He is the One who draws someone down life's field into the Red Zone and across the line of faith. And, He knows the just-right way to help an individual grow.

At the same time, the body of Christ helps new believers learn the biblical principles that give them one spiritual victory after another. It's a process that transforms lives. In the next chapter several stories unfold that show how that happens when believers are prepared to share their faith.

Discussion Questions

1. When you first became a Christian, what steps for spiritual growth, if any, were you given? Did they help? Based on your personal experience, what recommendations or advice would you suggest for new believer growth?

2. Why is it important to provide resources to help new Christians grow in their faith? What are the potential repercussions if this area is neglected?

3. What benefits does a new believer receive by participating in a Bible-teaching church?

4. How important is it for a new believer to join a small group Bible study of like-minded Christians? Elaborate on the benefits of participating in such a group.

5. What would you do to help new believers find the right church home? What factors should be considered?

6. What does the statement "the goal is not only to get decisions, but also to make disciples" mean to you? Do you agree or disagree with this premise and why? What precautionary steps should be taken to make sure people become disciples?

7. Besides attending church services and joining a small group Bible study, what are some other ways you'd recommend for new Christians to grow in their faith?

10

Receiving More Touches

Tim Tebow is a Heisman trophy winner. He's already made a tremendous impact on the game of football with his Hail Mary passes and astounding runs. But his greatest legacy will come from sharing his faith. Tebow has been deliberate about doing that because he cares more about his spiritual influence than he does about football.

In his book, *Through My Eyes*, Tebow explained that:

> A legacy that left eternal fingerprints on the lives of others would be a legacy to be remembered in this world and the next. The legacy God intended each of us to leave has to do with the impact our lives have had on the lives of others whom He calls us to serve. It has to do with the difference our lives make in the world—in our families, with friends, at work, at school, with our coaches and teammates, and all those others around us. Our legacy should be about building in the lives of all those others, doing something for others that will not only last in their lives here, but for eternity. (p. 208)

117

Whether the audience is large or small, every Christian has a sphere of influence. And, within that sphere are those to whom we can impart a spiritual inheritance. Friends, relatives, and coworkers are being drawn into the Red Zone; they're ready to enter into a personal relationship with Jesus. All it takes is some teamwork with Christians who know what to say.

In football, the coach assigns more "touches" to those who are prepared. They're the ones he sends into the game. Spiritually, it's much the same. Our heavenly Coach arranges more divine encounters for those who are ready.

The thrill of knowing the valuable outreach skills of RZE is their applicability to a wide variety of situations. Spiritual touches on an airplane, in a gym, on the phone, and in a doctor's office show how.

On a Plane

When I boarded a flight from Southern California to New Jersey, I had no idea that an interaction of eternal significance was about to take place. After hoisting my bag into the overhead bin, I sat down and heard the two men next to me fully engaged in a conversation.

They were getting to know each other—one was a doctor, the other a scientist. Eventually these middle-aged guys figured out I was a pastor.

With that discovery, they both expressed their disdain for church. So, I used the Bridge diagram to show them the difference between "Church-ianity" and Christianity, between religious rituals and rules and a personal relationship with Jesus. Their issues with church revolved around men. Christianity is centered in Christ.

That made sense, so they started peppering me with questions that I rarely encounter: "Why should we believe the Bible came from God when men wrote it?" "What about other religions?" "What about the hypocrites?" "How can a good God allow evil?" (Note: Kenneth Richard Samples' book *Without A Doubt: Answering the 20 Toughest Faith Questions*, Baker Books, 2004, addresses these issues and more. Another resource is *Give Me an Answer* by Cliffe Knechtle, IVP Books, 1986.)

I did my best to answer these long-held questions, plus several others. The doctor appreciated my responses so much that he looked me in the eye and took a deep breath. After letting it out slowly, he spoke: "I just learned my mother is dying of cancer, and I don't know what to say to her."

"This can help," I said handing him and the scientist each a copy of the gospel booklet, *Would You Like to Know God Personally?* We reviewed it together, especially so the doctor could learn how to use the little booklet to lead his mom to Christ and give her the assurance of going to heaven.

Then, the doctor mentioned that his wife was an atheist. So we talked about how, for most atheists, intellectual arguments don't usually carry much weight. Most of the time people who don't think there is a God have experienced a personal and tragic trauma. As a consequence, the atheist concludes that *if a good, loving, and powerful God were to exist and He let this happen to me, then I must be of no value to Him.* It is much easier for an atheist to believe there is no God than that God does exist and rejected her.

That explanation made sense to the doctor, who said his wife had suffered repeated sexual abuse as a child. So I told him that God had nothing to do with that. The further people move away from God, the more evil they become.

"What happened to your wife was so evil, it broke God's heart," I said. "He has even promised to exercise vengeance on those who do evil" (see Romans 12:19).

Then, I said, "Satan wants your wife to blame God and turn away from Him. In doing that, she is turning away from the only one who can heal her heart and rebuild her life. She needs to know that God loves her, and had nothing to do with that evil. She needs to see her situation from God's perspective so she can turn to Him for healing and rebuilding."

Our interaction helped the doctor come to the realization that he couldn't help his wife or mother until he personally turned to Christ and received Him. "You can't impart what you do not possess," I said. "However, once you receive Christ, God will help you talk with your mother." The doctor told me that he'd pray that same night.

Then the scientist quietly spoke: "Last year my best friend died. I was with him; he was only 35 years old. I'm a scientist and deal best with facts and empirical data. I don't know how to view this whole thing of life after death."

By then the Gospel had been shared a couple of times, so I reminded him that Christ rose from the dead proving that He was God, and there was life after death. I quoted some of the promises Christ gave about eternal life and said that "the minute we close our eyes here on Earth, we will open them in His presence in heaven." The scientist liked that. Then I underscored the importance of beginning that relationship by praying and asking Christ into his life. This time I added, "But the prayer needs to be sincere; from your heart to God's heart."

He responded saying, "I have prayed every day for the last six weeks. I thank God for the day and all my friends and ask Him to help me. Is that an okay prayer?"

I reassured him that it was a great prayer. "It was sincere, in your own words, directed to God, thanking Him and asking Him to help you. All you need to do now is invite Christ into your life and the relationship will become even more personal," I said. The scientist assured me, he was going to do that.

By listening to their intellectual questions and addressing them the best I knew how, these strangers opened up about their deepest personal, spiritual concerns. Inwardly they had already been seeking God's help. They were in the Red Zone, but needed some assistance to move closer to the goal.

Our discussion enabled me to point them to Christ. As I reflected on our long conversation, I realized they didn't even question any of the answers I gave to their tough questions. It was evident that the Holy Spirit gave me the words and answers I needed.

At the Gym

Melissa, a 25-year-old customer service representative, had been through the How To Share Your Faith training at her church. The first night I asked everyone to write down the names of those they wanted to share the Bridge diagram with. Thoughts of Anthony immediately popped into Melissa's mind. She'd already started talking with him about the Bible, so Melissa knew he was in the Red Zone. She prayed for him often and daily texted him a Scripture verse. When she forgot, he'd text a reminder.

Melissa said, "God was definitely tugging at his heart and I felt like, if I didn't take the opportunity to invite him into a personal relationship with Christ, who would?"

Before leaving class, Melissa told others in the group that she planned to see Anthony the next night. "We all got in a circle and specifically prayed for him," said Melissa. "At the time I thought, *really God? Can this work? Can I really be used to lead my friend to Christ?*"

The next evening, while at the gym, Melissa kept waiting for a providential opening, but it never came. She became discouraged and when it came time to go home, Melissa thought *"Great—I'm leaving and nothing happened."* Melissa started toward the door, then abruptly turned around and said "Hey, Anthony! Can I show you this cool thing I learned?"

He said, "Sure."

Melissa said: "I sat down at his desk, took out my notebook, and started to draw the Bridge diagram. When I asked Anthony if it made sense, he said 'yes.' So, I asked 'where do you see yourself?' He pointed to the left side of the divide, opposite God."

Then, he said, "I'm trying to figure out how to get to other side."

"Really?" Melissa squealed with excitement. She could hardly believe the diagram had worked and her friend was about to enter into "an amazing, wonderful eternal relationship with God."

Once Melissa regained her composure, she used ESPN to describe the benefits of what happens when someone receives Jesus into his life. She also let Anthony know that all it takes is a simple prayer from his heart to God's, then offered to lead him if he liked.

But when Anthony looked around the gym and said, "That's okay," Melissa realized the timing wasn't good. So she told him not to worry; he could say the prayer himself whenever he was ready. She said, "I shared a little of my testimony with him and let him know that I got saved in my bedroom, and he could too."

Later that evening, Melissa texted Anthony saying,

"I shared with u 2nite because I truly care about ur soul. I'm not good with my words but God has big plans for u. Just wanted to let u know I'll be here for u if/when u decide to enter into a personal relationship with God."

Anthony texted back saying,

"U r good with ur words and btw, I said the prayer. Nite."

Melissa was ecstatic. She said, "If the angels in heaven were cheering for him, I think I cheered just as much. I felt overwhelming praise to God for using me to invite someone into His kingdom."

On the Phone

Suzie was a newcomer to our church. One day I called to thank her for coming to visit. I also wanted to ask if I could answer any questions to help her feel more at home with us.

During our conversation, Suzie shared that her previous church experience, years earlier, had not been great. She felt like she was just going through the motions of religious activities. When it became clear that Suzie didn't have a personal relationship with Jesus, I explained the difference between, what I call, "Church-ianity" and Christianity, between religious rituals and a personal relationship with Jesus.

"Church-ianity is spelled 'D-O,'" I said.

Then I went on to explain how there is a God with a standard of right and wrong. But we have messed up and fallen short of his standard. Because we feel a sense of shame about that, we try to *DO* good things to make up for all the bad things we've done. That is the *DO* system—go to church, give money, volunteer to serve, and on and on.

The problem with that approach is that we never know when we've done enough to be okay with the Almighty. It's like running a race with no finish line.

The other problem is we frequently step out of bounds and make more mistakes. Each one increases the negative side of our account. It means we need to DO more good things to make up for all the bad things. Church-ianity is the *DO* system. It does not bring peace with God or within ourselves. Quite often all the *doing* becomes so frustrating that people drop out of church.

"In contrast," I told Suzie, "Christianity is spelled 'D-O-N-E.'"

What we could not *DO* for ourselves, Christ has *DONE* for us when he died on the cross. The penalty for our bad works is not good works; the penalty is death. The Bible says, "The wages of sin is death." But that is why God sent Christ to us. Jesus came to pay our debt and did that by dying on the cross.

The last thing Christ said on the cross was, "It is finished." In other words, it is DONE. The penalty for our sin was paid in full for those who believe in Him. Three days later He rose from the dead and went to prepare a place in heaven for us. He offers us forgiveness for our sins, a personal relationship with Him and eternal life. All of that is a free gift.

But He won't force us to respond. God made us free agents, not robots. He wants a love relationship with us, a relationship that we can choose to be involved in or not. So He knocks on the door of our hearts, but He waits for us to respond by praying and inviting Christ to come into our lives, forgive us, and begin to lead us. Once we do that, He promises to be with us forever.

Despite being in her garage, leaning on a broom, Suzie listened carefully. When I asked if my explanation made sense, she said "yes." She wanted to receive Christ right then, so I led her through a prayer to receive Christ.

A couple of weeks later, I met with Suzie to help her start growing in her relationship with Jesus. It's been several years since then, and she has led many Bible studies and continues to serve our church in significant ways.

In a Doctor's Office

An old football injury from UCLA followed me for many years. Several neurosurgeons had said I'd have to learn to live with the pain in my back. But Dr. Patel, a spine surgeon at UCLA Medical Center, finally gave me hope. He was convinced surgery would substantially reduce my discomfort.

At my first post-op appointment, I asked about his spiritual background.

"I give back through my profession," he said.

"Yes," I replied, "and you do very well with that. I know your work pleases God. But He wants to give something to you: forgiveness, eternal life, and a personal relationship."

"Everyone has his own way of pleasing God," the doctor said. "Mine is to give back through my job."

"Yes, but no matter how many good things we do, we still fail, mess up, and need forgiveness," I said. "That is where Christ comes in. In all the religions of the world, there is no forgiveness for man's sin apart from the cross of Christ. God offers that forgiveness as a free gift. We only need to recognize that reality and ask Him to forgive us."

Though Dr. Patel seemed to enjoy our conversations, I didn't sense any spiritual progress—until months later.

When he entered the exam room, he seemed happy to see me. His dark eyes sparkled when he said that he'd seen my name on the appointment list and couldn't wait to talk to me. He wanted to share something not related to my surgery. Then he pulled out his smart phone and showed me a picture of his five-day-old baby. Richard was his first child. "A gift from God," the doctor said with a grin.

That gave me an opening to say I, too, had a gift for him. But first I wanted to share some thoughts that arose from our previous conversation. "I've wondered if you'd want to know if something you believed was *not* true? I think you might. Something isn't true just because we believe it. First we must figure out if it is true. So, we study the evidence and the facts and then come to a conclusion about its validity. If the evidence confirms that something is true, then we believe it."

"A doctor does this in his profession all the time," I explained. "You find out the history of a problem, do a physical exam, order the x-rays, MRI, discogram, and perhaps consult with others. Once all the evidence has been collected and analyzed, then you decide what to believe based on the weight of it."

Then, I encouraged him to do the same with Christianity. "Look at the facts and make your decision on what to believe based on the weight of the evidence. These three books can help with your research." I handed him:

The Case for Christ by Lee Strobel. After graduation from Yale Law School, Strobel became the legal editor of the *Chicago Tribune*. When his wife became a Christian, he (an atheist) started examining the credible evidence that Jesus is the Son of God. As a result Strobel became a committed believer who has dedicated his life to informing others about Christianity's validity.

More Than a Carpenter by Josh McDowell. Thinking that Christians must be "out of their minds," McDowell argued against their views. But eventually he realized his arguments didn't stand up against the evidence. He speaks and debates professors on university campuses all over the world.

So What's the Difference by Fritz Ridenour. This book examines how other faiths differ from biblical Christianity and what those differences actually mean.

Though the doctor was extremely busy, he accepted my challenge to read them. Then he surprised me by asking me to autograph the books. Though I wasn't their author, I was delighted to write: "To my favorite doctor, Dr. Patel. May your search lead you to the most wonderful discovery of your life—a personal relationship with the God who just gave you your first child, Richard." Then I signed my name.

Though I still haven't heard the rest of the story, there's no doubt God was with me when I pointed Dr. Patel toward Christ. Nor do I doubt God was and is reaching out to him and will use other people and influences along the way.

On Life's Playing Field

God has placed people all around you who are in the spiritual Red Zone. Nothing is more thrilling than being a part of the Lord's work in a person's life. And, nothing is more satisfying than being part of God's eternal plan to draw people into His kingdom.

Learning what to say and practicing will prepare you for whatever opportunities God brings your way. Sometimes you may use the Bridge diagram, sometimes you may not. But having a specific message well in mind will equip you with the confidence and boldness necessary to share your faith. By leading others to Christ, you'll be building a legacy worth cheering about. May God grant you one touch after another.

Discussion Questions

1. Do you believe that every Christian has a sphere of influence? What does this mean as it relates to evangelism? Describe your sphere of influence?

2. Do you agree that our heavenly Coach arranges more "touches" or divine encounters for those who are ready? Why or why not?

3. How has God used you in the life of a non-Christian since beginning this discussion group.

4. What's the difference between "churchianity" and "Christianity?" How might you use these comparisons in future spiritual interactions?

5. As you complete the study of this book, how has your confidence level changed regarding sharing your faith? On a scale from 1–10, how confident do you feel? What number did you assign yourself at the beginning of this study? How has this number changed and why?

6. Share with your group your hopes and dreams for how God might use you to reach out to non-believers in the coming days, months, and years. Describe the spiritual legacy you hope to leave.

7. Spend time praying as a group. Pray specifically for those in your sphere of influence who are drawing near to God. Ask Him to open the doors for meaningful and ongoing spiritual conversations. And, thank Him for what He will do in and through you as a result of your taking the time to learn and practice RZE!

About the Authors

Dr. Kent Tucker loves God and people. His passion to help seekers come to know their Savior and become fully devoted followers of Christ began developing while Tucker was a student at UCLA through his involvement with Campus Crusade for Christ.

After receiving his Masters of Theology at Dallas Theological Seminary, then a Doctorate in Ministry at Fuller Theological Seminary, Dr. Tucker filled associate and senior pastor roles for more than 40 years. During this time, he continually explored the most effective ways to teach believers how to share their faith.

In 2006, Dr. Tucker became the founder and president of How To Share Your Faith, an equipping ministry that trains believers to lead people to Christ. Since then churches in 49 states and 15 countries have started using his video curriculum. Dr. Tucker conducts evangelism-training seminars and conferences all over the country. He lives in Rancho Cucamonga, CA with his wife, Betsy. They have two adult children and three grandchildren.

Patti Townley-Covert helps Christian nonprofits maximize their message and empower their prose in ways that broaden their audience (see *PTCovert.com*). A former executive editor, she's won several Evangelical Press Association awards for her articles and work with in-house publications. Townley-Covert has been published in numerous magazines, journals, and books. Since 2010 she's written a monthly feature on individual nonprofits for the *Christian Examiner* newspaper. In addition, she's the communications director for Transform LA, a catalyst for personal and societal transformation through networking the body of Christ in the greater Los Angeles area. Townley-Covert lives in Ontario, CA and has two adult sons.

Garry Poole wrote *In the Red Zone's* discussion questions. He is a strategic planning consultant, a speaker and trainer, and author of numerous resources including *Seeker Small Groups.* As Willow Creek Community Church's key evangelism leader for eighteen years, he is the innovator of seeker small groups and strategist of creative outreach initiatives. Poole has offices in Chicago and Denver, and consults at churches and corporations around the world.

"It's simple, clear and easy to learn. I highly recommend it."
—LEE STROBEL

Finally!

A **FREE** App that Makes Sharing Christ Easy

Interactive Voice Narration Multilingual

Made in the USA
Monee, IL
22 July 2020